UKRAINE DIARIES

Also by Andrey Kurkov

Death and the Penguin

The Case of the General's Thumb

Penguin Lost

A Matter of Death and Life

The President's Last Love

The Good Angel of Death

The Milkman in the Night

The Gardener from Ochakov

Andrey Kurkov

UKRAINE DIARIES

Dispatches from Kiev

*Translated by Sam Taylor with an afterword
translated by Amanda Love Darragh*

Harvill Secker

LONDON

Published by Harvill Secker 2014

2 4 6 8 10 9 7 5 3 1

First published with the title *Ukrainisches Tagebuch* in 2014
by Haymon Verlag, Innsbruck-Wien

First published in Great Britain in 2014 by
HARVILL SECKER
20 Vauxhall Bridge Road
London SW1V 2SA

A Penguin Random House Company

Penguin
Random House
UK

www.vintage-books.co.uk

www.penguinrandomhouse.com

A CIP catalogue record for this book is available from the British Library

ISBN 9781846559471 (paperback)
ISBN 9781473520479 (ebook)

Penguin Random House supports the Forest Stewardship
Council® (FSC®), the leading international forest-certification organisation.
Our books carrying the FSC label are printed on FSC®-certified paper.
FSC is the only forest-certification scheme supported by the leading
environmental organisations, including Greenpeace.
Our paper procurement policy can be found at:
www.randomhouse.co.uk/environment

Typeset in Scala by SX Composing DTP, Rayleigh Essex
Printed and bound by CPI Group (UK) Ltd, Croydon, CR0 4YY

Publisher's Note

Ukraine became independent from the USSR in August 1991. Reports of vote-rigging in the 2004 presidential election, allegedly won by Viktor Yanukovych, led to the Orange Revolution, and Viktor Yushchenko became president. Yanukovych was, however, victorious in the 2010 elections. Owing to a lack of growth mired by corruption in Ukraine, Yanukovych sought economic ties with both Russia and the European Union.

On 21 November 2013, the Ukrainian government suspended negotiations on the EU Association Agreement. This agreement called for closer trade links, political and economic reform, and the release of ex-Prime Minister Yulia Tymoshenko, who was imprisoned in 2011 on charges believed to be politically biased. Russia opposed the agreement, and threatened to impose harsh trade restrictions on Ukraine and to increase gas prices if it were signed.

Kiev, central and western Ukraine are more pro-European; the east is predominantly pro-Russian. The south is a mix of pro-European and pro-Russian. The Maidan protests, described in these pages, involve a diverse group of anti-government protesters; political parties of the opposition; and later self-defence groups set up to protect protesters from pro-government mercenaries. The main opposition parties are Batkivshchyna (centre-right; Tymoshenko's party, led by Arseniy Yatsenyuk); UDAR (centrist, led by Vitaliy Klichko); Svoboda (right-wing, led by Oleh Tyahnybok); and groups which emerged during the revolution, such as Pravy Sektor (far-right nationalist, led by Dmytro Yarosh).

Yanukovych's party, the Party of Regions – the ruling party as these diaries begin – is made up of various groups with different ideological and political views, ranging from centrist to pro-Russian.

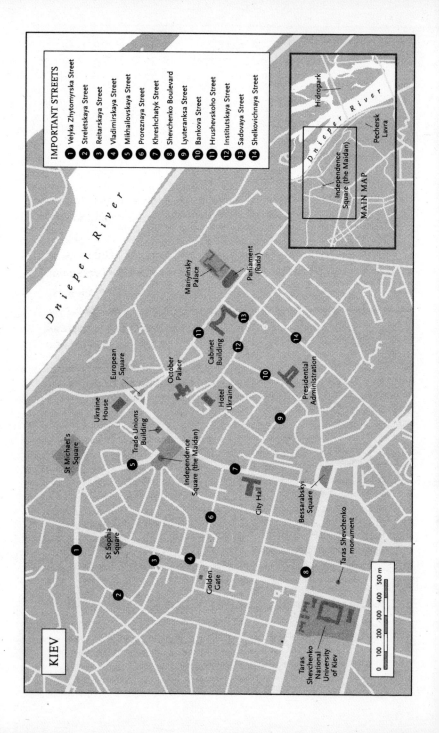

Preface

When nothing in particular happens in the life of a man and his country, the man might believe his existence to be stable and eternal. In fact, that life – where time is measured in career changes, in the purchases of new houses or cars, in family gatherings, in weddings and divorces – truly is stable. The man who lives in one of the world's 'hot spots', or who simply lives next to an active volcano, has a different view of time. The worth of each day, each hour experienced, proves infinitely greater than that of a peaceful week. When you live next to a volcano, real or metaphorical, the day is filled with so many events that it proves physically impossible to remember them all. These events inevitably end up in the history books, sometimes comprising only a few lines, sometimes one or two pages.

I now understand why, when I was at school, I much preferred reading the private diaries of writers or politicians who had witnessed history to reading actual history books. I remember the diary of the great Russian poet Alexander Blok, covering the years 1917–18. I remember Franz Kafka's diary, and I remember in particular the diary – which I read recently in its complete version – of the famous Ukrainian film-maker Alexander Dovzhenko, in which he would sing the praises of Stalin or revile the Jews and the Ukrainians, just in case he was arrested and the KGB read his notebooks, so he would be able to point out these passages as proof of his loyalty to the Soviet regime.

I have kept diaries for more than thirty years. Several times, my Ukrainian editors have asked to publish them, even if only fragments of them, but until now I have never been able to force myself to extract from these private writings anything I was ready to share with readers.

And then, having been led on more than one occasion into the path of a whirlwind of history, I found myself the witness to the dramatic events that arose in November 2013 in Ukraine, events of which we have not yet seen the end. I do not know what will happen next, or what lies in store for me and my family. I only hope that everything will be all right.

I am not leaving. I am not shying away from reality. I live each day in the very centre of reality. All five of us – myself, my wife Elizabeth, and our children Gabriela, Theo and Anton – continue to live in the same apartment, in the heart of Kiev, five hundred yards from the Maidan Nezalezhnosti, Ukraine's Independence Square. From our balcony we have seen smoke rise from blazing barricades, we have heard the explosions of grenades and gunshots. Life goes on, throughout all of this; not once has it stopped. And I have recorded this life almost every day, so that I can attempt, now, to recount it to you in detail. A life in times of revolution, a life spent waiting for war. A war that, as I write these words, seems terribly close, closer than ever.

Thursday 21 November 2013

Tonight, around midnight, a meteorite fell on Sevastopol. Why there in particular? Pure chance, probably. But still, that it should choose to land on the most Russian city in Ukraine, whose picturesque bays are home to Russia's Black Sea Fleet!

I would not have paid any attention to this nocturnal event, had there not appeared today a declaration by the prime minister, Mykola Azarov, announcing the suspension of preparations to sign the Association Agreement with the European Union. In one of my novels I described a secret factory, hidden away in the Ural Mountains, which produced artificial meteorites. The dream of the Soviet military's high command: bombarding the United States with artificial meteorites, while making people believe they were real ones. So I wondered if this meteorite was really a natural event, or if it had not been a way of proclaiming to the most Russian city in Ukraine that negotiations between Viktor Yanukovych and Vladimir Putin over the renunciation of our country's Association Agreement with Europe had ended successfully (for Putin).

Closer ties with Europe have been abandoned. Now, we are going to love Russia again.

Europe is apparently in a state of shock. Me too. Did Yanukovych really have to spend six months announcing that 'we are walking towards Europe'? Did he really have to gather his parliamentary group in September at the regional party headquarters, traditionally installed in the Zoryany cinema, to ask each person there to walk with him, in an orderly fashion, carefully keeping pace, and to suggest to all those who refused to follow him that they should leave the group and the party?

We did not have to wait long for the people's reaction to Azarov's announcement. This evening a crowd began to gather in the Maidan.* In the meantime, there had been more news: the Foreign Ministry joyously declared that it was no longer dangerous for Ukrainians to go on holiday in Egypt. In other words, any of you who were thinking of going to Europe, catch a plane to Egypt instead, and who cares if you get massacred, accidentally or on purpose, by local Islamists or other revolutionaries. This makes me feel sick.

That said, the way this is being staged is absolutely classic: Azarov announces the decision not to sign the treaty on a day when Yanukovych is out of the country. He is in Austria, where he is already busy reassuring Europe: 'We'll sign the agreement with you, just not right now.' And he adds that he has no intention of liberating Yulia Tymoshenko.[1] If Yanukovych were a three-headed dragon, at this moment each of the three heads would be travelling separately but acting in perfect sync. If one of them were in Moscow, the Muscovite Yanukovych head would be giving a completely different speech, one that did not even mention Europe.

This afternoon, abandoning the next chapter of my Lithuanian novel, I went to the Yaroslavna and ordered a coffee. Five or six minutes later, I added 50ml of Zakarpatsky cognac to it. It didn't make me feel any better. There was no one in the cafe I recognised. Customers came in, looking gloomy, and I was tempted to think that they too knew that Europe was now no longer going to enlighten Ukraine. But maybe they were worried by altogether different problems, their own private problems, of far less importance.

---

* The Maidan, a word of Persian origin, was originally the square in eastern cities where the market was held. In Kiev it was renamed Independence Square in 1991, after the fall of the Soviet Union.

Back at home, I went on Facebook. People were calling for a gathering in the Maidan to demand that the treaty be signed. They advised to take warm clothes, rugs, a flask of tea and a supply of food for the night. I simply didn't have the strength to go. I didn't feel like it either. I don't feel like anything any more. Not only that, but the television screen showed Putin grinning from ear to ear while the speaker declared in a somewhat strange voice that Russia is delighted to develop its collaboration with Ukraine. What collaboration? A three-year trade war, with embargoes on the export of, first, cheese, then meat, then Ukrainian beer, and so on? Not to mention the constantly postponed co-production of Antonov aeroplanes.

The world seems to have gone mad this morning. In Alchevsk, blue water ran from the taps. A Swiss tourist entered Georgia, perched atop a camel, an animal from which he has not been separated for more than thirty years. His name is Roland Veron, and in Tbilisi he was given an award for the most original traveller. I wonder if they gave the camel anything.

Here, everything is simpler and sadder. We have, once again, had our future taken away from us.

Friday 22 November

Vilnius. The temperature here is no more wintry than it is in Kiev. The conference on Ukraine and its European future was not cancelled, in spite of the Ukrainian prime minister's declaration. Though it's true that the Polish president, Bronisław Komorowski, and the Lithuanian president, Dalia Grybauskaitė, have pulled out, along with a few other top-level European politicians. As for me, I have to talk about the country's future after the treaty.

This evening, a gala dinner was organised at the Kempinski Hotel restaurant, but it didn't improve the morale of those of us from Ukraine. At the next table sat the first president of Lithuania, Vytautas Landsbergis, the former Ukrainian president, Viktor Yushchenko,[2] and his brother Pyotr, a former member of Parliament. While Landsbergis talked about European values, Yushchenko used his speech to criticise Yulia Tymoshenko again. After which he gave a little pot of honey to everyone at his table.

While this was happening, people were spontaneously gathering in Kiev for a protest in the Maidan, in spite of the rain. Someone had brought a large tarpaulin to make a shelter for the protesters. Straight away, the police turned up and confiscated the tarpaulin. A man in plain clothes read out a court decree banning the erection of any tents, kiosks or other 'small architectural forms' during the period from 22 November to 7 January. At the same time, the city police representative announced that the protesters would not be removed.

Viktor Yanukovych still intends to come here, to the Vilnius

European summit. The Polish and Lithuanian politicians at the conference cautiously hypothesise that the Association Agreement will be signed in spite of everything. They think Azarov's declaration is motivated by excessive EU pressure regarding the Tymoshenko affair.

Well, I agree on that point. For Yanukovych, Yulia Tymoshenko is the principal – and most dangerous – enemy. If she were liberated, her popularity would soar again and she would become the sole leader of the opposition, relegating the three white knights of today – Oleh Tyahnybok, Vitaliy Klichko and Arseniy Yatsenyuk – to the background.

Azarov intervened again today, this time with a supposedly reassuring speech in which he claimed the refusal to sign the Association Agreement did not mean he would instead be signing a treaty with Russia about Ukraine's entry into the Customs Union. In fact, the majority of our country's inhabitants know nothing about these two unsigned treaties and simply believe that an Association Agreement with the EU would lead Ukraine into Europe, while a treaty joining the Eurasian Economic Community Customs Union would place us once again under the economic and political influence of the Russian Federation.

Today, in Kiev, the second European Cup for knife fighting began. Teams from Russia, Ukraine, Lithuania and Italy took part. I didn't even know that knife fighting was a sport!

Monday 25 November

Vilnius, 1.40 a.m. It's raining. According to my taxi driver, it is supposed to start snowing around 3 a.m.

After midnight, European diplomats asked me the question: 'What should we do with your country?' I replied: 'What should you do with it? Take it! And take me too, along with all its other inhabitants. Ukraine has already had new masters. The important thing is that the new rules should be comprehensible and easy to implement. That's what everybody wants. And that each of those rules should be one line long, forming a single and unique proposal. Like the Ten Commandments: You shall not kill, full stop. You shall not steal, full stop. Etc. So the Ukrainian citizen will lift his hands to the sky and say: "Oh, how simple this is! How easy it is to live in a civilised manner!" And then, just in case, the citizen will ask: "But will the local police officer also have to obey these rules?"'

If everyone accepts the rules, the poor police officer will find himself bound by them as well. If we don't accept them, he will maintain the right to take ice creams for his children from the local kiosk without paying for them. And so the kiosk owner's children will grow up hating the police officer.

Goodnight to all the local police officers, to all the businessmen, to everyone who takes part in this life!

Yesterday, there was the biggest mass protest the Maidan has known since Yanukovych became president. The procession of people in favour of closer European ties left the monument to the poet Taras Shevchenko at noon and walked to European Square. The police counted 20,000 protesters. In Russia, the television news talked of 'several thousands', but the opposition claimed that more than 100,000 people came together to protest against the government. During the rally, speakers called for the president's resignation and a government reshuffle.

After two hours of successive speeches, one of the orators suggested they stop talking and start acting – by setting up camp outside the Cabinet. On the way, the protesters split into three groups. The biggest headed for the Cabinet building, the two others for Parliament and the presidential administration building. Clashes immediately occurred between the protesters and the *titushky*,[3] who, along with the men of the Berkut – the special police of the Ministry of Internal Affairs – surrounded the ministerial building to protect it. The procession's belligerent vanguard was composed of members of the Svoboda Party and aggressive young people who, having smashed open the entrance barrier, attempted to breach the line of defence. Truncheons and flagpoles entered the fray. The Berkut began throwing stun grenades. The Svoboda activists constantly shouted nationalist slogans that had nothing to do with the cause of these protests. Yuriy Lutsenko, the former Minister of Internal Affairs in Viktor Yushchenko's government, was trying hard to stop the fighting, inviting everyone to return to the Maidan and then to come back to the Cabinet the next day. Finally, the Svoboda activists agreed and returned to European Square, where the party members began putting up tents to create a protest village.

The Party of Regions was not inactive either. During Saturday night and Sunday morning, they constructed a stage on Mikhailovskaya Square for a rally and installed a row of dry toilets. They were preparing to make the square a base for their supporters.

On Sunday night, students put up ten tents in the centre of Lviv and raised the flag of the European Union. In Cherkasy, the police prevented them. The police are now guarding the central squares of many cities in Ukraine. An opposition speaker called on the protesters not to disperse before 29 November, the date when the European summit in Vilnius is due to end.

Because of the protests, the day to commemorate the victims of Holodomor[4] went unmarked. It was the governor of the Donetsk region who suddenly remembered it. In his brief speech, he acknowledged that the great famine was entirely planned, because during that period, in the parts of Ukraine that belonged to Romania and Poland in 1932 and 1933, no one went hungry. One wonders if he will now suffer the wrath of the Party of Regions, to which he belongs, and who deny any responsibility on the part of Stalin and the Communist Party of the Soviet Union in the famine that caused the deaths in Ukraine of between three and five million people.

Tuesday 26 November

Today, at 2 a.m., the administrative court of Odessa issued a decree prohibiting the organisation of all rallies and protests on twenty-five squares and streets in Odessa, as well as on 'all adjoining land'. In other words, the entire city is now forbidden to protesters! At 5 a.m., court bailiffs arrived, holding this decree in their hands, at the base of the Richelieu monument, and began knocking over the tents that the Euromaidan supporters had erected there. These tents sheltered a total of twenty-four people. Three of them, including Odessa's Euromaidan leader, Alexei Chorny, were sentenced to five days in prison for 'uncivil acts' and resisting law enforcement officers. The court that gave Chorny five days banned journalists from attending the trial, and sentencing took place in camera.

I am increasingly convinced that the entire Ukrainian legal system has not only entered the shadowlands, like the country's economy, but has sunk into a deeper darkness. There are more and more legal judgments made in the middle of the night, when the country is supposed to be asleep. If the judges who are working nights are sleeping during the day, we can be somewhat reassured as to their mental health. But if they are working twenty-four hours a day, it has to be doubted whether they can even remember the judgments they made one hour earlier. And anyway, as has been proved on several occasions by journalists, judges have been handed judgments written in advance without their agreement, already unsealed and signed. This is, in any case, how they deal with opposition representatives – and, indeed, with anyone who is unhappy with the authorities and does not conceal their feelings.

In Kharkiv today, almost two hundred people gathered in the central square. They were here the night before, with gauze strips on their mouths like gags. The local authorities immediately banned all mass protests and rallies, justifying this measure by claiming it was taken against the risk of an epidemic of flu or other contagious diseases. The city truly is sick: in 2004, at the time of the Orange Revolution, its inhabitants were much more active.

Putin's statements on Ukraine keep coming. In the latest, he said that Ukraine owed Russia $30 billion. Last week, the debt was, I believe, only $18 billion.

Today in Kiev, students declared a general strike. Those from the city's university gathered around the monument to Taras Shevchenko, and from there marched towards the Maidan. Almost two thousand others joined protesters in the square.

In the evening, in European Square, *berkutovtsy* – Berkut agents – attacked three opposition deputies with truncheons and tear gas, even after they showed identification. So it looks as though the police have already taken away the immunity from arrest guaranteed to members of Parliament by the constitution – or at least to those who support the opposition.

Protesters who had come from Lviv to take part in the rally in the Maidan complained on the Internet that there had been too few European symbols and flags. There were not many Ukrainian flags either. Most of the flags on display were those of the opposition parties. While writers and journalists were speaking, the public listened attentively. But as soon as they were succeeded by opposition politicians, who clearly did not agree on a joint plan or message, the rally was transformed into a sort of dry run for future presidential elections. It is true that the appearance of Yuriy Lutsenko, who spent a year in prison on the official orders of Yanukovych, did arouse the crowd's interest and attention. But he was talking about himself, not about any particular party. At one stage, the supporters of Yulia Tymoshenko invited protesters to march on the Cabinet building. Result: those who responded to this radical call found themselves clashing with the police who surrounded said building and tested the effects of rubber truncheons on the protesters' bodies.

The previous night, in Dnipropetrovsk, *titushky* destroyed the tents erected in the local European Square by protesters. Everyone found inside them was beaten up. The leader of the local Euromaidan was evacuated in an ambulance, suffering from traumatic brain injury and multiple contusions. Euromaidan organisers in the city banned the flags of political parties from rallies – only European flags would be accepted.

In Donetsk and Luhansk, it appears that nothing is happening. In Crimea too, all is as calm as a graveyard.

'Protesters' kits' have gone on sale on the Internet. One of the ads reads: *For sale, complete equipment for protesters. Includes everything required by a person preparing to defend his interests and opinions during the cold season. The kit contains a half-litre Thermos flask, a cooler bag, an umbrella, a floor mat, a waterproof poncho, a sleeping bag, a portable phone charger, a water canteen, a small gas camping stove, food rations for three days, four thermochemical hot-water bottles, and a protester's guide with summaries of relevant articles of law in the event of a conflict with police. Total price: about 1,000 hryvnas.* Recently, an instruction manual for drivers has become very popular: *How to Behave with Transport Police Officers.* It also contains many reminders of the laws and regulations that policemen routinely break when arresting drivers on the road.

Sinister weather today. Not a single ray of sunlight the whole day. Sometimes rain, sometimes sleet. In conditions such as these, there is nothing like a sauna to perk you up. Perhaps I will have that pleasure tomorrow, if all goes as planned.

Wednesday 27 November

It's freezing. Yesterday, I finally put winter tyres on my car. I bought a meat pie from a nearby bakery run by Uzbeks and I went to see my mother in hospital. I stayed in her room for half an hour. She showed me photographs of Murka, her cat, who's in the house with my father. She had forgotten that I was the one who went to their house especially to photograph Murka, whom she misses so much. Back at the apartment, I made pumpkin soup and meat for dinner.

Putin is waiting for Ukraine to collapse. Yanukovych says he won't turn the country away from the path leading to the European dream, and at the same time he will refurbish secondary roads. Out of the blue, he declared that these minor roads are more important for Ukrainians than major roads. He probably means that their refurbishment is more important than closer ties to Europe. In principle, this is logical: if we take the wrong road, we will never reach Europe. We will break down on the way.

From the hospital ward of the prison where she is being held, Yulia Tymoshenko called for all the parties to unite in the struggle against Yanukovych. But the Maidanistas, meanwhile, are continuing to ban politicians and their flags. In Lviv, protesting students chased the Svoboda Party deputy Yuriy Mikhalchishin off the stage at a rally, after he invited them to remember the 1918 Battle of Kruty – when a detachment of Ukrainian students fought a division of the Red Army – and to march boldly to their deaths in the name of Ukrainian ideals. Once he understood that the students did not want to hear him, he declared that these protests were organised by the Yanukovych administration. Why do politicians have such difficulty imagining that people can go out on their own and protest when something in the government gets them angry? Everyone can see that these Maidanistas have united spontaneously, that they do not belong to any particular political party. But now the opposition parties are taking turns trying to lead these people! Of course, unaffiliated Euromaidans are something very new.

The administrative court in Kiev suddenly issued a decree ruling that the abandonment of closer ties to Europe is invalid. Presumably the session took place during the day, not the night. Admittedly, the decree does stipulate that *only the president, or the person authorised by the president to this end, can terminate or begin international negotiations.* In other words, if Yanukovych officially gave Azarov instructions to suspend the signature of the agreement, then there is nothing that can be done about it. But if Azarov acted independently of the president, which the latter seems to me to be implying, then there is nothing to prevent Yanukovych sending Azarov packing and signing the Association Agreement himself in Vilnius tomorrow. All the more so as the president's office confirmed that he will, in spite of everything, attend the summit. I mean, why would he go, if not to sign the agreement? Just to add to his collection of enemies?

Today in Kharkiv, a birthday was celebrated: that of Yulia Tymoshenko. This was how I learned that she is already fifty-three years old. The doors of the hospital where, according to your point of view, she is either being cared for or imprisoned, were decorated with flowers, slogans, and Ukrainian and European flags. Tymoshenko's fellow campaigners built a stage in front of the hospital, intending to wish her happy birthday through loudspeakers. About five hundred people turned up. There was a huge heart made of red roses mounted on a wooden pedestal painted in the colours of the European flag. Instead of the usual banners demanding 'Freedom for Yulia!', this time most of them proclaimed 'Freedom for Ukraine!' Access to the hospital itself was blocked by police, and the roads approaching it were controlled by traffic police.

A line of students from the Polytechnic Institute of Kiev marched from Victory Square to the Maidan. Behind them was a bus filled with Berkut agents. The students were demanding permission to take part in rallies instead of attending classes. In western Ukraine, many universities and colleges are already on 'political holidays'. In Kiev, only students from the Mohyla Academy, the national university, are allowed to protest instead of going to classes. The Education Minister, Dmytro Tabachnyk, today threatened to cancel the grants of any students who take part in the rallies.

As for the students, they are organising cultural activities in the Maidan. They have already planned the screening of films and concerts by young musicians, as well as installing a crate for bookcrossing. They are asking people to bring in particular books by Ukrainian writers and to write in each of them *In memory of Euromaidan*. The rule is simple: if you want to take a book to read, drop one of your own in the box.

Putin has finally revealed how he bought Yanukovych: a new promise to lower the price of gas to $270 for a thousand cubic metres, a preferential loan of $15 billion and, once again, the co-production of Antonov aeroplanes! I am getting déjà vu: I have heard that promise before somewhere.

Thursday 28 November

President Yanukovych has set off for Vilnius, but why is he going to the European summit? It's a mystery. So much so that his supporters lugged the coffin of European rapprochement through Kiev, wrapped in the flag of gays and lesbians. The anti-European campaign organised by the chimerical – or rather, virtual – social movement Ukrainian Choice has become ridiculous and exasperating. Posters and signs have been put up all over the country with images showing that all Ukrainians, after the signature of the Association Agreement with the EU, will become homosexuals. Even in the metro, each time you take an escalator, you have to pass dozens of these posters. In Kiev, this propaganda campaign is considered laughable, but I am afraid that in the east and in the provinces, people will naively believe that universal conversion to homosexuality is the condition imposed by Europe on Ukraine for the signature of the treaty.

Putin reminded us again today that Ukrainian banks and companies owe Russian banks more than $30 billion. And that's without counting government debts. Russia is continuing its economic war against Ukraine. Today it banned the importation of Ukrainian porcelain.

Snow fell during the day, but it melted on contact with the ground. In the Maidan, some five thousand students arrived in an orderly fashion. In the evening, Slava Vakarchuk, singer with the rock band Okean Elzy, went onstage to encourage the people gathered there not to give up, not to despair, even if tomorrow in

Vilnius Yanukovych does not sign the Association Agreement. He wanted to slip away after his short speech, but the crowd shouted out: 'Sing! Sing!' And so, without musical accompaniment, in chorus with the thousands of people at the rally, he launched into 'Get up, my darling, get up!'

In spite of everything, the country is not getting up the way it did to protest against the falsification of the presidential election results in 2004. This is not a new Orange Revolution. It is simply the refusal to bury the European dream. In the south and in the east, that dream simply does not exist. For Donetsk and Sevastopol, Europe is too distant. It is much closer for western Ukraine,[5] for Lviv, Ternopil, Ivano-Frankivsk and Chernivtsi. That is why people there are up in arms, while in eastern Ukraine all is silent.

Friday 29 November

Ukraine is up shit creek. The European summit ended happily for Moldova and unhappily for us. Ultimately, Yanukovych did not sign anything. So why did he go to Vilnius? To be photographed with Angela Merkel?

But Kiev is the scene of a new rally. Or, more precisely, the Party of Regions' anti-rally. Dozens of buses are parked in Glory Square and elsewhere. From there, citizens brought in mostly from eastern Ukraine, the majority of them *byudzhetniki* – government workers – brandishing Ukrainian flags, march towards European Square where a stage has already been set up, decorated with the ruling party's two favourite colours: blue and white. The rally has a name: 'For Europe in Ukraine'. While Maidanistas are championing Ukraine in Europe, this group is doing the opposite. All the speakers repeat the same message: that it is too early for Ukraine to become part of Europe, that it is still too small, too weak, too poor. It can enter the Union when it is big enough and rich enough to talk as equals with both Russia and Europe. The leader of the Party of Regions' parliamentary group, Oleksandr Yefremov, states that Ukraine might yet sign the agreement with Europe, perhaps even this year, perhaps even in May ... The speakers declare that Luhansk, Donetsk, Kharkiv and Zaporizhia have been under ferocious pressure from Russia, and that consequently there is an urgent need to stop the process now and think it over more carefully.

The rally is gradually transformed into a concert, and plastic cups of tea are handed out among the crowd.

While this is happening, lines of *titushky* are forming near the Mariyinsky Palace: thousands of them, all dressed in tracksuits. Two journalists from a public television channel have gone there with a camera to find out what is happening. They are assaulted by about twenty people, punched and thrown to the ground, their camera smashed, their pockets emptied and a USB key stolen from them. The police advise them 'to steer well clear of *titushky*' and refuse to get involved. A little later, about 6.30 p.m., a group of *titushky* attack pro-European protesters in the Maidan. A fight ensues. Smoke grenades are thrown and the police suddenly arrive. The *titushky* disappear. Policemen in gas masks line up in a row and begin shoving the protesters towards the Independence monument. A second row of law enforcement officers form on the other side of Khreshchatyk Street, cutting the rally in two.

Later on, I flick through the television channels to check the news. Almost nothing about the Maidan. Instead the news is talking about another fatal assault on CIT security staff in Kharkiv. This is the sixth time in a few years that an armoured truck has been attacked. People were killed, and the murderers are being sought, but there is little chance of them being found. More and more often, I hear the theory that the criminals who attack CIT security staff in Kharkiv are working for Russians. The Russian border is less than twenty-five miles from the city.

Saturday 30 November

In the old days, Soviet schoolchildren used to learn about Bloody Sunday in their history lessons. Now, Bloody Saturday has been added to the contemporary history of Ukraine. Very early this morning, about 4 a.m., police special forces committed a massacre in the Maidan. The mobile phone network was cut while there were several hundred protesters in the square. They were sleepy, and to begin with they didn't understand what was happening. All of them were beaten with truncheons: students, elderly people, everyone. Those who tried to save themselves were caught, thrown to the ground and beaten with sticks. A group of students, men and women, cornered in a dead-end street, began to sing the Ukrainian national anthem. They sang it while they were punched and kicked and dragged to waiting police vans, which took them into custody. Some of the protesters escaped towards St Sophia Square and St Michael's Square. They ran faster than the *berkutovtsy*, who were slowed down by their knights' armour, but who pursued them all the same.

When the protesters stopped at St Michael's Square, a very small monk hurried towards them and invited them to take refuge in the monastery. He told them that the doors were open and that the abbot had given them permission. More than a hundred protesters – most of them youngsters – hid inside St Michael's Golden-Domed Monastery. They barricaded the door from within. In the morning, Kievites brought them tea, food and warm clothes. The police turned up and attempted to enter the monastery, but the people wouldn't let them in. Kiev's chief of police stated that the order to attack the protesters had been given because they were preventing the decoration of the New Year tree in the Maidan.

Results of Bloody Saturday: thirty-seven arrests, thirty-five injured taken to various hospitals in Kiev. But that is probably not the definitive tally. The list of the disappeared is being drawn up now. Rumours abound that people were killed last night and their bodies taken to an unknown location. The city is overcome with grief and fear. All the faces you see on the streets are gloomy. The television news announced that on the ninth day the police had put an end to the protest movement. The young people taking refuge in the monastery say they do not intend to go home, and that after this morning they are no longer afraid of anything.

During the day, a deputy from the Svoboda Party, Ihor Myroshnychenko, declared that the reason the police had managed to remove the protesters from the Maidan was because there were no politicians there. Yes, nine days of protest without the involvement of any party, even an opposition party: that's a new record.

Of the main television channels, only 1+1 showed a true picture of what happened. On the same channel, the news gave a brief account of a visit paid by several opposition members to the students in St Michael's Monastery. The students were not too thrilled by this meeting. One of them asked: 'What about you? Why weren't you in the Maidan last night?'

The European Union and the United States condemned the police's violence towards the protesters. The smell of menace floats in the air.

Sunday 1 December

I came home from the Maidan about 11 p.m. Apparently there is going to be a raid tonight. This evening, the Maidanistas stormed Bankova Street. They took a bulldozer, thronged with activists waving Ukrainian flags, and attempted to knock over the police vans that were barring access to the presidential administration building. The *berkutovtsy* launched a counter-attack. Enter Klichko – the former boxing champion and leader of the centrist UDAR Party (*udar* means 'punch' in Ukrainian) – who asked everyone to go back to the Maidan, shouting that it was this kind of provocation that would allow Yanukovych to declare a state of emergency in the country. Nobody listened to him. Petro Poroshenko, the former Foreign Minister under Yushchenko, who also attempted to stop the assault on the presidential administration, was quite simply pushed aside. Result: Berkut agents attacked the Maidanistas and pillaged the Writers' Union building, where several journalists – men and women – were taking refuge. They smashed the ground-floor doors and windows and dragged the journalists outside, where they continued beating them up. Ukrainian, Polish and Georgian journalists showed police their press cards, thinking that this would protect them. But the *berkutovtsy* took the cards off them and then beat up the journalists even more while yelling insults at them.

On Institutskaya Street, I passed dozens of protesters covered in blood. Some were taken to the Maidan, where large tents were being put up. Svoboda and Batkivshchyna activists went from Bankova Street to the Maidan and seized the Trade Unions building, breaking down the doors and claiming it as the Maidan's headquarters. Kiev's chief of police handed in his resignation. It looks as if the government's power is crumbling, which means that the declaration of a state of emergency is entirely possible.

A line of seventy vehicles driven by pro-European activists went to Mezhigorye to blockade the residence of President Yanukovych, but the police barred their way, parking a bus crossways to form a sort of barricade.

I have just heard that forty buses transporting student officers from the internal armed forces, followed by various riot control vehicles – including water cannons – have left Kharkiv and are headed towards Kiev.

On Channel 1, the latest newsflash announced that the clashes in Bankova Street have left a hundred policemen injured. One wonders how the bulldozer borrowed by revolutionaries was able to reach Bankova Street. Journalists who were there are reporting that, although the protesters who took part in the assault on the presidential administration were chanting slogans in Ukrainian, they were shouting at each other in Russian. Poroshenko also claimed it was an act of provocation. Lutsenko heralded the beginning of a revolution. A revolution during a state of emergency? It seems unlikely. More like a guerrilla rebellion. Indeed, those who believe the Maidan cannot force the government into concessions are talking more and more about guerrilla tactics.

Monday 2 December

The Maidan held firm. There was no police raid. At 2.30 p.m., I had a meeting with Gaby's form teacher, Galina Petrovna. We had tea at the French bakery on Yaroslaviv Val Street. Strange that she is defending Gabriela, who doesn't want to work and is doing all she can to skip classes. Galina Petrovna asked me to take a look at the script for the school play to celebrate the bicentenary of Taras Shevchenko's birth. She begged me to persuade Gaby to take part in the play and to act the role of one of the heroines in the poet's life.

There has been no confirmation of the rumours of mass resignations by deputies from the ruling party. Inna Bohoslovska is scaring everyone by repeating that Putin wants war. After the scandal of the saucepans – which the owner of her former residence accused her of stealing but she denied – it is very difficult for me to take her seriously on TV talk shows. Apparently she is the only one yet to have quit the Party of Regions. Her husband, it is true, has stayed.

Parliament has promised to study the question of the dissolution of Cabinet tomorrow, but police have not confirmed the declaration made yesterday by the prime minister announcing the resignation of Kiev's chief of police.

In Lviv, Lesya Gongadze has just been buried. She never lived to see the funeral of her son, who was found decapitated in 2001 and remains unburied.[6] In Kharkiv, there were the funerals for the CIT security staff killed in a robbery. Yanukovych acknowledged that Berkut agents, under his orders, 'had demonstrated excessive zeal' in beating up protesters and journalists. And the mayor's office stated that it had not asked the police for its support to decorate the New Year tree in Independence Square. In Donetsk, there was supposed to be a rally in support of Yanukovych today, but it was cancelled. Perhaps they didn't manage to gather enough *byudzhetniki*, or perhaps the master of the Donbas region[*] – the oligarch Rinat Akhmetov – had his say.

In Kharkiv and Dnipropetrovsk, *titushky* laid into pro-European protesters. Meanwhile, the Crimean Parliament demanded Yanukovych declare a state of emergency.

The occupants of the Maidan spoke to Kievites in the centre of the city, asking them to disable their Wi-Fi passwords so that the protesters could use the Internet in the streets. And my computer in Vladimirskaya Street shows that several of my neighbours have indeed opened up access to their networks.

In the evening, almost 20,000 people gathered in the Maidan. As for me, I took the train to Kamyanets-Podilskyi. I have several meetings planned with students and readers in Kamyanets, Uzhhorod and Lviv.

---

[*] The Donbas region covers the eastern provinces of Donetsk and Luhansk.

Tuesday 3 December

A cool, sunny day. Slavko Polyatinchuk welcomed me at the station and drove me to the Sem' dnei Hotel ('Seven Days' Hotel). The hotel manager offered me a room for free. The mayor's office is just next door. On the roof: the flag of Europe, a circle of stars on a blue background. It is like a different country here. In front of the mayor's office is a small square surrounded by a park, with an empty rostrum. The pro-European protesters gather here every day from 2 p.m. onwards.

When I got there, after my meeting with the university's students, several processions of students from the professional schools converged on this square, waving flags in the colours of their institutions. Two local politicians arrived to test the microphone and the sound levels. The atmosphere was perfectly normal and peaceful. No police anywhere in sight.

In Kiev, on the other hand, the Parliament building is currently protected by sixty special forces buses. The main entrance is closed. Around the building, which is encircled by a tight band of *berkutovtsy*, are several thousand protesters. The deputies enter through an underground passage, the entrance to which is on Sadovaya Street, probably in the building opposite which shelters various parliamentary commissions. Might there also be underground passages leading to the presidential administration, located half a mile away, and to the national bank? I wonder why the deputies did not use this tunnel to escape Parliament last year, when the building was under siege by Afghanistan veterans protesting against plans to cut their tax reductions? Back then, the deputies removed the badges from their jackets and escaped through the service exits at the back of the building.

Azarov told Parliament that there was no more money in the state's reserves due to the pro-European protest movement. How strange! Before, he always said that it had been his predecessors who were to blame: Yushchenko and Tymoshenko.

Police have begun legal proceedings against participants in the motorised protests organised to support the Euromaidan. That is why, this evening at 7 p.m., those protesters are gathering on the Naberezhnoe road, on the riverbank, near the monument to the founders of Kiev. They are inviting legal experts, human rights campaigners and journalists for a debate about how to defend their rights in the courts.

Meanwhile, in front of the presidential administration, thousands of protesters shouted: 'Get the jailbird out!' The former jailbird, Yanukovych – he was convicted twice in his youth, allegedly for rape* and definitely for assault and battery – has left on an official visit to China, where he plans to stay until 6 December. On his schedule, there are more than twenty contracts and agreements to be signed. He has been accompanied by a delegation of Donetsk businessmen and oligarchs that he has in his pocket, as during the visit there will be a 'forum of representatives from Chinese and Ukrainian business interests' at which he is supposed to speak. While his house is burning down, he's being invited for dinner and making his plans for the future!

Officials from the Kiev mayor's office continue to worry themselves sick over the biggest New Year tree in the capital. This has now been transformed into a propaganda object, covered with

---

* All documents about arrests and investigations were destroyed while Yanukovych was governor of the Donetsk region, so it is now impossible to be certain about this.

posters attacking the president and his cronies. The mayor's office is promising Kievites that instead of one main tree in the centre, they will be able to put up their own tree in each district, so they will have somewhere nearby to celebrate the event. I cannot ever remember such an arboricultural frenzy gripping the city! And the deputies from the Party of Regions are accusing the opposition and the Maidan protesters of trying to 'steal the New Year celebrations from the children'.

The deputies have ensured the failure of the vote to dissolve the Cabinet. Azarov remains in power. As soon as it was clear that the regionals had won again, Azarov announced that the force was not with the Euromaidan. Well, yeah, with a Parliament like this, there's not much chance it will be. This morning, the channel TVI was taken off the air as a punishment for its honest perspective on the protest movement.

Apparently, all mobile phone numbers within the bounds of the Maidan are recorded on a special machine. Today, the protesters received strange welcome texts from unknown numbers: *I believe in peace and stability! I support the New Year with a tree and a Father Christmas, not with rallies and fights!*

Vladik, one of my cousins, bought a new SIM card that he uses whenever he goes to the Maidan, leaving his old mobile phone at home. He says that is what he was advised to do by his friends working for the SBU – Ukraine's security services.

Thursday 5 December

It snowed last night in Kamyanets-Podilskyi. Slavko Polyatinchuk accompanied me to the bus station and waited until my bus left for Khmelnytskyi. By 9 p.m., I was there. I had four hours to wait before the departure of my train to Uzhhorod. I spent two hours on my laptop in a cafe, then I went to the station. There were about twenty people asleep in the waiting rooms, most of them elderly. Several clearly homeless. Gypsy children aged around twelve ran between these rooms, looking for victims they could nick something from. I noticed that they were watching me too. Finally, I got on the train, climbed into the upper bunk and fell asleep straight away.

In Uzhhorod, I was welcomed by Oksana, a university student. She took me to a cafe near the station and we were joined by Misha Roshko, who is a writer and also a dean at the national university of Uzhhorod. We talked about the day's schedule. We cancelled the meeting with history students, due to the fact that the rector had given them political holidays to take part in rallies. In fact, Misha told me, the students who live in other towns and villages simply went home, taking advantage of the situation. But the meeting with the philology students took place, as did my speech at the municipal library.

There were not many people in the central square, though students from the Carpathian university of Augustin Voloshin were there – so not everyone has deserted the city. There were also some from the Theological Academy, holding banners. A few orators spoke in a jerky, incoherent way, ending with the words '*Banda, guet'!*' – which means 'Get out, crooks!'

In Kiev, protesters organised a picket line in front of the Public Prosecutor's office to demand the liberation of people held in custody. Apparently one of the protesters beaten up and arrested by the police has a damaged eye and needs an urgent operation. The people taking part in this protest erected two tents outside the building and swore they would not leave until they had been given what they demanded. Vitaliy Zakharchenko, the Minister of Internal Affairs, declared that police would no longer strike protesters. He has no intention of resigning, but promises an internal investigation. For now, legal proceedings have started against three policemen for 'abuse of authority', and against sixty-four protesters. How very fair and balanced!

In the city, car stickers of the European flag are now for sale, intended to be placed above the Ukrainian flag that features on Ukrainian registration plates. Traffic police have already warned that they will issue tickets for this, as the stickers make it difficult to read the number plates. Kiev's policemen now have eyes only for cars' registrations.

On the stage at the Maidan, the singer Ruslana[7] promised to set fire to herself if the government refused to listen to the protesters and sign the Association Agreement. In other cities too, the movement is becoming more radical. Except in eastern Ukraine, of course.

Friday 6 December

I arrived in Lviv at 6.30 a.m. The city welcomed me with snowfalls. Oksana Prokhorets was late due to snow and ice on the roads. We went to her house and ate breakfast. The day passed very quickly. Despite the bad weather, there are many pro-European protesters and they are highly active. The majority are students and Svoboda supporters.

Ukrainians have already collected 500,000 hryvnas for public television. I think Channel Five and TVI may well be banned from broadcasting in the next few days.

Yanukovych, we have learned, does not want to come home. He has landed, not in Kiev, but in Sochi, where he is drinking tea with Putin. We have no information about the results of his trip to China, only rumours. For example, it is said that he agreed to lease land in the south of Ukraine to the Chinese. But those rumours have been circulating for a year already, with others claiming he had signed an agreement for the immigration of several tens of thousands of Chinese people into Crimea.

In the evening, the news is given that even after Sochi, Yanukovych is not returning to Kiev, but will fly to Malta for an official visit. Later we learn that the Maltese government has refused to receive him, so he has no choice but to head home. More than three hundred cars driven by protesters go to Boryspil airport to welcome him back.

Saturday 7 December

I got off the train this morning, and was home by about 8 a.m. I didn't wake anyone.

Today is Anton's birthday: he is eleven years old already!

At one o'clock this afternoon, his friends came to our apartment and we all went to the Hidropark. We found the Paintball Planet club fairly quickly, and there we all put on our outfits and masks and picked up our guns. We divided into two teams, the Greens and the Blues. We each tied a headscarf in our team's colour around our neck. Then we spent almost two hours shooting paintballs at one another. It was cold outside. We took regular breaks and went inside the club building to warm up and drink cocoa from a vending machine. When we ran out of ammunition and the battle was over, we went home to eat pizza. The party ended at 7 p.m. Everyone was happy, especially the birthday boy. Only one of Anton's friends was slightly upset: he hadn't put his mask on properly and, during the first battle, he got hit on the lip by a paintball. After that, he didn't want to take part any more. But a couple of the club's employees took him to the shooting range and, once he'd calmed down, he practised knocking over beer cans.

Today, the police and the Berkut sent reinforcements to protect the television centre on Mechnikov Street, as well as the television tower. The Maidanistas say they plan to mount a demonstration there, to protest against the government's information policy – it has to be said that the main television channels' news programmes are completely silent on the protests – or to stop them broadcasting.

An activist from Road Control,[8] Andrey Dzindzya, has been arrested. In Cherkasy, there are clashes between pro-European protesters and police. In Donetsk, there are finally protests against the government. Many people think that Yanukovych has already signed an agreement with Putin for Ukraine's entry into Russia's Customs Union. But this evening, a member of the Russian government stated that there was no agreement of this kind and that the subject had not even been discussed during the meeting, the previous day, between the two presidents. It's hard to believe that.

Sunday 8 December

Kiev was in turmoil all day, and in the evening there was a minor earthquake: Svoboda members in balaclavas threw a lasso around the neck of Lenin's statue, on Shevchenko Boulevard, and pulled it off its pedestal. Immediately they began reducing it to dust by smashing it with sledgehammers. They started with the head. Many of them, as well as a few passers-by, picked up pieces of red marble as souvenirs. A bus full of *berkutovtsy* came and parked nearby, but they did not get out of the vehicle. What happened to the Communists who constantly guard the monument? Their tent was right there next to it. They probably ran away.

In the Maidan, nearly 100,000 protesters gather. I am one of them. We shout: 'Azarov, resign!' This chant fades as we applaud a procession of cars that has driven from Kharkiv to support the Euromaidan. We learn that more than five hundred people have come to Kiev in this way and that they intend to stay in the Maidan until we are victorious. The *veche* – the popular assembly – begins, as usual, with a prayer. Cardinal Lyubomyr Huzar speaks first, then the singer and poet Taras Petrynenko interprets sacred songs.

In front of the Mariyinsky Palace, the government holds its own meeting: they bring two thousand *byudzhetniki*. For a long time, nothing happens, and then they look as if they are about to leave the park. They are stopped by the announcement that Azarov is going to make a speech. But apparently he decides not to address his paid protesters.

Monday 9 December

In spite of everything that is going on, I did make a speech for the launch of Yuliya Pilipenko's* autobiographical novel, *Ginger*, at the Cinema House. She came to Kiev just for that. There were seven people in the audience, which, given the situation, can be considered a huge success!

The day began quite peacefully.

At 9 a.m., a free hairdressing salon opened on the first floor of the city hall occupied by the protesters. Volunteer hairdressers snipped the locks of whoever asked. There was soon a line of customers. But not everyone managed to get their hair cut because soldiers with metal shields closed off Hrushevskoho Street, then the Berkut launched an attack against the picket lines that protesters had set up near the Cabinet and Parliament buildings. Several vans full of soldiers sealed off the Maidan from European Square. Berkut agents swarmed from buses near Bessarabskyi Market. The police ordered restaurant and shop owners to close their doors and send their employees home. The three central metro stations were also closed; we suspect they have been mined. Passengers were evacuated. Trains no longer stop in the centre of the city.

At his home in Mezhigorye, Yanukovych gathered together the *siloviki* – the main enforcers of law and order – and then promised

---

* Yuliya Pilipenko, twenty-eight, had a kidney transplant ten years ago. In 2007, she became world tennis champion in singles and doubles at the World Transplant Games in Bangkok.

a round table and declared that he would speak on television, with the three previous presidents.

And he did speak. I thought it was a vile spectacle. When he talked about the students who'd been beaten up in late November by Berkut agents, it looked like a satisfied smile played across his face. The first president, Leonid Kravchuk, appeared to be smiling too. Only Leonid Kuchma seemed visibly uncomfortable. Yushchenko wore an indifferent expression, as if he wasn't really there.

Impossible to know what is happening at the moment in the Maidan.

Wednesday 11 December

The barricades were demolished last night, on Lyuteranska Street, Bankova Street, Institutskaya Street and Hrushevskoho Street. Earlier that evening, I had walked back home from the Masterclass cultural centre, after an event organised by the French Institute. It was cold and the streets were deserted. The Pechersk Lavra, with its church sitting above the door to the subterranean monastery below, looked like the backdrop to a historical film. But when I arrived at the Arsenal metro station, I discovered an enormous, Soviet-era war machine, like a cross between a bulldozer and a tank. I don't know why it had been brought there – to destroy barricades or to smash holes in the walls of houses? Further down on Hrushevskoho Street, next to the Officers' House, a pile of public benches formed a first barricade. A second was in the process of being built, this time from broken furniture, metal dustbins and anything else they could find. There were a lot of people huddled close to braziers.

In front of the barricade stood the soldiers of the Berkut; behind it, the defenders of the Maidan, and some people who had simply turned up to discuss politics with them. Among this last group were a few women, whose voices stood out incongruously against this backdrop in revolutionary colours. Further on, beyond the barricades, there were more soldiers.

When I turned the corner at the Officers' House, I saw a narrow passage between the wall formed by the shields of the *veveshniki* – the soldiers from the internal forces – and the side of the building.

A small rally was taking place close by. A woman spoke to the soldiers through a megaphone: 'I am a mother of five.' The men watched her with weary eyes.

A little further on, in Institutskaya Street, there were yet more police, but arranged in a column this time, and ready – so it seemed – to get going. The head of the column was turned towards the Maidan. I took photographs while I walked. But this morning, the barricades had gone and there was nothing on the news about clashes with police, injuries or arrests. Strange.

Friday 13 December

I returned from Lutsk with the poet Pyotr Korobchuk and Mykola from the publishing house Tverdynia ('Fortress'). We went to my house for breakfast, then we went to the Maidan. It was a cold, sunny day and we were in a good mood. First we stopped at the square on Proreznaya Street. I took a photograph of my guests sitting on the seats in the shapes of coffee cups designed by Konstantin Skritutski. We passed the barricade at the junction of Proreznaya and Khreshchatyk, and there, at the back of the tent village, we found people dressed as cartoon heroes: the panda from *Kung Fu Panda*, and the squirrel from *Ice Age*. The panda talked to us about what was happening, and the fact that his kids at home often yell '*Panda, get*'!', a childish paraphrase of the slogan '*Banda, get*'!' – 'Get out, crooks!' – which is chanted a thousand times a day in the Maidan.

We had our photographs taken with the guy in the panda outfit. There is no longer a set price for this kind of picture. 'Give what you can,' he said. Mykola gave him ten hryvnas, and so did I.

In the Maidan, we spotted the tent from the Volhynia region. Pyotr and Mykola had a photo taken in front of their compatriots' tents, then we set off to explore the square. It was full of tourists, all enjoying the sunshine and taking pictures of each other against a backdrop of revolution. Lots of Russians among them.

A travel agency in Krasnodar, I have learned, is organising tourist excursions to the Maidan, and apparently it's going well. All the Moscow–Kiev tickets have been sold. It has been a long time since we were the centre of such attention. Russian celebrities fly here to have their photos taken in front of the barricades. We have already seen the television presenter Kseniya Sobchak and the stylist Sergey Zverev.

While I was away, barricades have been put up in Institutskaya Street and near the TsUM (Central Universal Department Store). True, it's not a difficult thing to do, if you have time. The people fill bags with snow and large chunks of ice taken from the pavement, and hoist them to the top of the construction. They are now well over twelve feet high, maybe even fifteen feet. Admittedly, no one has attempted to break through, in spite of our fears and the government's threats. It has not happened yet, but it will sooner or later: policemen and *berkutovtsy* continue to swarm on Kiev, coming from Donetsk, Rivne and other regions. For now, the atmosphere in the Maidan and on Khreshchatyk Street is festive, almost like a carnival with all these pandas and squirrels.

The Russian Orthodox Church has once again spoken out against the Maidan, this time through the mouth of Archpriest Andrey Tkachev, leader of the St Agapit Church. The simplest thing is to quote him in full: 'Such a manifestation of anarchism does not, on the whole, please me. Because, for us, democracy is not direct; it is parliamentary, representative. If not, we have to destroy all the foundations of our state. I have never had representatives in power in all the twenty years of this country's independence. That does not mean that I should go to the Maidan and yell. I will not go, and I will not let the children go, because it is futile. I do not bless anyone who goes to the Maidan. Because I do not believe that a million people with limited ideas will create the right decision simply by virtue of numbers. Once again, the question is asked of this country's citizens: do you want to join Europe, or do you want to build communism in one country? In the same square are gathered people who simply want Europe, those who do not, and those who want something else altogether. They have only one point in common: they are all against the government. But anti-establishment minds do not produce anything creative.'

I wonder what creative thing the Russian Orthodox Church is going to produce.

Yesterday, the television broadcast the round table organised by Yanukovych with the aim of national reconciliation. The Ukrainian students were represented by a big, rosy-cheeked lad who went on about Europe and turned out to be a member of the Young Regions, the youth division of the Party of Regions.

This evening, the snow gave way to a fine, gentle rain. The temperature must have risen. Not too much, I hope. Otherwise the barricades will start to melt, and that could lead to a police attack.

I have poured myself a small glass of gin and tonic. I will drink it, and then to bed. Goodnight, my country!

Saturday 14 December

We went to Silpo today, the supermarket in Borshchagovka. We did our shopping there, for ourselves and for Grandma Raya and Grandpa Yura. Then we went to see them.

My mum complained about my dad, as usual. He broke the headphones again, which he uses to watch television every night. At three this morning, he was watching it with the volume turned as high as it will go. That woke her, and she had it out with him in the living room. She was worried he would wake the neighbours. My brother promised to come round and repair the headphones. Nothing new. Apparently this is not the first time that these headphones, which have a ten-foot lead, have been damaged. During my conversation with my father yesterday, however, I had the impression that his hearing was improving. His deafness is sometimes selective: he hears only what he wants to hear. I remember how he never used to hear the questions my brother and I asked him about his communist beliefs.

We stayed about an hour and a half with Grandma Raya and Grandpa Yura, then we went home. I attempted to get back down to work on my Lithuanian novel, but I didn't write anything. There is a heaviness in my head that makes my ideas seem as clumsy as a tortoise.

Monday 16 December

Yesterday, students carried onto the stage at the Euromaidan a three-foot-high model of Yanukovych's ear and demanded that he listen to the protesters. If he doesn't, they promised to give him a new brain. In 2010, during the presidential campaign, all the posters of Yanukovych showed him in a thoughtful pose, with his political credo emblazoned beneath in large lettering: *I will listen to each of you!* In the space of three years, he has clearly not heard anyone or anything.

Ruslana, the journalist Mustafa Nayem and many other Maidan activists have been summoned by the Public Prosecutor for interrogation. Yanukovych says he has found the three 'extremists' responsible for the first cleansing of the Maidan. They are the former KGB officer Vladimir Sivkovich; the leader of Kiev's local authority, Oleksandr Popov, who is so fond of New Year trees; and the leader of the presidential administration, Andriy Klyuyev. I seriously doubt they will be sentenced, though they have been 'suspended from their functions'.

Tomorrow, the Maidan activists intend to put 'trees of blood' in front of Klyuyev's office, decorated not with tinsel and baubles but with photographs of the protesters beaten up by the Berkut in November.

Not irrelevantly, the government announced a new rise in salaries, which are already much higher than normal, for judges. Clearly, they will be expected to hand down severe sentences – prepared in advance once again – for protesters and opposition representatives. Let us hope they make enough money doing this to buy a house abroad, where they can take refuge when Yanukovych's time in power comes to an end.

Today at 2 p.m., there was a meeting of the jury for the Country's Pride Awards. They gave us documents about the 'national hero' candidates. My favourite is a 95-year-old country doctor who continues to visit his patients in neighbouring villages – even in winter, even when it snows – on his bicycle! The jury will meet one more time, and then, on 27 March, the prize ceremony will take place in the Ivan Franko Theatre. Assuming, of course, that the situation in the country has not worsened by then.

Tuesday 17 December

Yanukovych flew off this morning to meet Putin, and this afternoon he announced that the price of gas delivered to Ukraine was going to be reduced by 30 per cent. So that is the price of giving up our European future. One wonders what else will become cheaper thanks to Putin's goodwill. Human life here already has an aspect so low that it could hardly fall any further.

Ruslana was interrogated by the Public Prosecutor for five hours! What can you talk about for five hours with a prosecutor? Presumably he spent all that time asking the same question over and over and Ruslana refused to answer. Then he got tired, and the singer was released until the next interrogation. Life is becoming more and more like those old Soviet films where intelligence officers questioned by the Gestapo remain stubbornly mute. Glory to the heroes! To the old ones in Soviet films, and to the real ones in Ukraine today!

Wednesday 18 December

Bath day. Or rather, bath evening. We had a good time in the steam room. Each of us drank two pints of tea and a glass of *cha-cha*. We met at the sauna at 6 p.m. We discussed the political situation in temperatures of 100 degrees Celsius. Then the historian and journalist Danylo Yanevsky arrived, and he banned us from talking about politics in general, and Tymoshenko in particular, in order not to ruin the sauna's positive effects on our state of health.

I walked home, passing by the Maidan. There, around campfires, people were talking about the latest news from Moscow. Apparently, the new agreement on the price of gas has a clause that enables the Kremlin to revise the price every three months. Depending on Yanukovych's behaviour. I imagine that's not the only interesting bit of small print in that contract.

A guy who had been arrested near a brazier, next to the Independence monument, said that he went up to a policeman this morning and asked him if it was true that they were no longer allowed to hit protesters. The policeman showed him his rubber truncheon and very kindly answered him: 'They talked about us not hitting people, but they gave us truncheons. And when you have a truncheon in your hand, what are you going to do? You're going to use it!'

Yes, it's the same thing as giving everyone machine guns and ammunition and telling them not to shoot.

In Russia, Pussy Riot have been freed, and Nadezhda Tolokonnikova immediately broke the news on Facebook. Moscow is 'democratising' in preparation for the Winter Olympics. If that is the case, they'll be releasing others too. Maybe even Khodorkovsky![9]

Euromaidanistas and antimaidanistas continue to do their thing. Sasha Irvanets, writer and pro-Maidan activist, went to Kharkiv to give a speech. I didn't go with him, even though the poet and writer Serhiy Zhadan asked me to. I have neither the desire nor the strength to appear onstage and play at being a politician.

The antimaidan activists always complain that they are not given the money they were promised for taking part in the protests. However Andrey, from Lazarevka – where we have a country house – said that people in the village bring not only money but also warm clothes to the Maidan. Kievites continue to supply thousands of jackets and sweaters, dropping them in various places, so that anyone who needs them can dress warmly. Two or three days ago, I saw an old lady carrying hand-knitted socks and offering them to guys near the barricades in Hrushevskoho Street. The first one she spoke to said he already had two pairs.

Friday 20 December

A fine snow, like flour, has been falling since this morning. The boys didn't want to go to school. As for Gaby, she left late and we didn't even know if she would get to school.

Barely ten days until New Year's Day. The country is waiting for Russian money. Krasovitsky, the publisher, came here yesterday evening. He stayed for half an hour and then escaped for a meeting with a person who has connections with the Ministry of Finance: the state owes him 4.5 million hryvnas.

The country will begin 2014 renewed, winning and losing, still stirred by a month of turmoil. In any case, it has all provided Ukraine with weeks of free publicity on all the television channels in the world.

In the space of a year, two new words have been invented: *titushky* and *Euromaidan*. Just like *perestroika* and *glasnost* under Gorbachev.

European Square was sealed off by a row of buses today, with hundreds of anti-terrorists deployed: the four presidents, we learned, were praying together at St Vladimir's. To whom were they praying? And to ask for what? Were they asking God to make the Maidan disappear? Or, more modestly, for a loan, as long as it was for more money than the one promised by Putin?

Monday 23 December

Sunny, 3°C. We went for a walk yesterday – Natasha Kolomoytseva and I – in the Hidropark. Natasha is an old family friend. On the banks of the Dnieper, absorbed by our conversation about the political situation, we drank a small bottle of Ukrainian Greenwich cognac, then we had a coffee near the metro, and went our separate ways.

I went to see Petya Khazin. We talked until 10.30 p.m. After that, I intended to go straight home, but I decided to walk down Khreshchatyk Street. In front of the city hall, I bumped into Taras Kompanichenko, who was with some musicians from the group Khoreia Kozatska. They were going inside to play for an audience of revolutionaries. I followed them, sat down, and listened. I had a brief conversation with the man who had been reciting Shevchenko's poetry and waving a portrait of the poet from a stick, like a flag. On the other side of the flag was that famous verse: *Borytesya – poborete*, 'Fight, and you will win.' Then I walked at a leisurely pace to the Maidan – so leisurely, in fact, that it was midnight before I got home.

Tuesday 24 December

Yesterday I wrote a new chapter of my Lithuanian novel, a scene that takes place in the house of a Russian oligarch, near London, for which he has ordered enormous bulletproof armchairs. I was pleased.

At 5 p.m., I went out and caught the trolleybus to go and see my old friend Sasha Milovzorov, an artist and gallery owner in Shevchenko Square. For more than an hour, I listened to life during rush hour, the conductor yelling as he tried to convince people not to crowd into the vehicle but to wait for the next one, which would be along very soon and completely empty. But no one believed him, and they kept cramming themselves into the trolleybus.

After that, I went to the sauna at 6 Kobzarskyi Passage. Sasha Milovzorov and Valera-the-engine driver were already there. We drank beer and chatted. We discussed the fact that Valera needed a brand name for his model trains, which, apparently, comply with international collectors' standards and are constructed at a 1:15 scale. He was proud to have received $10,000 for his latest work, bought by the representatives of the Russian Railway as a present for their boss. One year's work, at a thousand dollars per month. We talked about tools, and then about the past, and that was how we learned that Valera had long ago been parachuted from Russia to straighten out a *sovkhoz* in the Kiev region. He was a livestock specialist. He immediately sent two hundred old cows to the abattoir – they were only providing ten pints of milk per day – and bought young ones. He began to develop the farm, and fell out with the *sovkhoz* manager, who from then on did his best to bring Valera down, by demanding that the board of inquiry intervene. The technician in charge of animal feed was constantly drunk, and it was impossible to find another one in that region, so in the end Valera was dismissed for being unable to manage his staff.

After the sauna, I helped Valera, who was slightly tipsy, into a minibus. And then I walked to the tram station in order to watch the departure and arrival of tram number 12, the tram of my childhood, which, when I was young, used to take me from Pushcha Vodytsa, where we lived at the time, to Kiev, passing through the forest. I even thought about getting in a carriage and riding the tram for a while, then taking it back the other way as far as Podil. But I had enough sense to content myself with simply watching one arrival and one departure. I took photographs of those two trams – one approaching, the other moving away. And then I took a minibus home. I was the only passenger.

Wednesday 25 December

As usual, for 'English' Christmas, the children stayed off school. In the afternoon we went across the road to Phil and Lada's new apartment – just about finished and looking fantastic, as you would expect from an architect. Christmas dinner was punctuated with improvisation games. For a couple of hours we were far from the madding crowd.

Thursday 26 December

Tatyana Chornovol was attacked last night. She was driving home on the road from Boryspil when she was chased by a Porsche Cayenne, which attempted to shove her car into the ditch. The Porsche finally managed to block her vehicle. Several men jumped out, dragged her from her car, and beat her violently before dumping her in the ditch. There were pictures of Tatyana in the newspaper in a dreadful state, practically disfigured. Eyes swollen, cheeks bruised, her whole face puffed up like someone allergic to wasp stings.

It has been announced that even Viktor Yanukovych is outraged and has ordered the police to urgently find the culprits by any means necessary. Police have opened an inquiry into the attack, with the expected charge being assault and battery (art. 296 para. 2 of the Penal Code). Vitaliy Zakharchenko, the Minister of Internal Affairs, said that three individuals who took part in the attack have already been identified, and two of them arrested. We await further news.

It's hard to imagine Yanukovych being overly worried by this beating though. After all, Tatyana Chornovol did illegally enter his private property and take photographs of his palaces so she could display them on opposition websites.

Police are also trying to clear up another big and scandalous crime. This one concerns the Maidan activists occupying the city hall, who are accused of stealing the baubles and tinsel stored in one of the building's rooms and intended to decorate the two real fir trees growing on either side of the main entrance.

It is time I started thinking about the New Year celebrations too. I can't possibly expect Grandma Raya and Grandpa Yura to take care of it, given their age and their poor health, so we will organise the party at our house. On the night of the 31st, I will jump in the car to pick up my parents. The next morning, I will take them back home, and we will go to Crimea for our winter holidays. There is a train to Sevastopol at one in the afternoon.

Friday 27 December

Recently, people have been offering free classes in English and self-defence in the Maidan for all those who aspire to a glorious European future. The classes take place every day at 9 a.m. and 4 p.m. at the Trade Unions building. There are only thirty people in the English class. That's not many. If we want to join Europe any time soon, we need to put more effort into learning foreign languages. I wonder how many people are going to the self-defence classes, and what they are learning.

The Trade Unions building already hosts the activities of the Maidan Open University, with speeches on public administration, the history of non-violent protest movements, Russia, and the state of public education in Ukraine. Activists have already seen Mikhail Ilyenko's film, *The Man Who Walked Through Fire*. Shame they don't display the programme of films on the door of the city hall. Even on the Internet, I have not seen the next showings announced yet.

Strange developments in the Tatyana Chornovol case. The police say they have reason to believe that the opposition itself organised the attack on the journalist, so they could then talk about the threat to press freedom! Klichko's brothers and other people are already being accused. And yet, among the suspects arrested so far, none of them have links to the opposition. Quite the contrary, in fact.

Road Control seems to have changed into the Maidan's mechanical cavalry, going under the name 'Automaidan'. Apparently almost every town in Ukraine has its own army of motorists, ready to participate in four-wheeled protests against the powers that be. Not bad! Even if, every night, all over the country, unknown people continue to set fire to vehicles belonging to the participants in these protests. Two nights ago, in my beloved Reitarskaya Street, a car was burned in front of the house next door.

Monday 30 December

Today in Donetsk, there was, in spite of everything, a gathering of pro-Europeans. They even organised a march through the city centre. They were watched every step of the way, of course, by Party of Regions members and a few plain-clothes policemen. At one point, a simple bystander, who was filming the procession's arrival, accidentally recorded a man giving orders into his mobile phone. The man said, 'Send our girls to meet them!' and ten minutes later a group of old, retired ladies rushed up to confront the Euromaidan supporters, yelling God knows what kind of pro-Russian bullshit. Others, who had gone around the procession, began throwing eggs at the protesters. I suppose we should be thankful they weren't stones. There was nothing very impressive about the protest: only about three hundred people took part. In a city with a million inhabitants, that is far too few to be taken seriously.

Wednesday 1 January 2014

I made a quick trip to the Silpo supermarket yesterday and bought what we needed for the New Year dinner. About 7 p.m., we put two geese in the oven and tidied up the apartment. At 9 p.m., I went to fetch my parents. It took my father a long time to climb to the third floor; he had to stop for several minutes on each landing. Asthma. Mum too had trouble with the stairs, but she went before Dad out of principle and was the first to reach the apartment door. Then our friend Natasha arrived with a salad and a cake. About 10.30, my brother's wife, Larisa, rang our doorbell. She brought two dishes: a Macedonian salad and a mimosa salad. Misha showed up soon afterwards. We got the geese out of the oven at 11.30. The children switched the television on. We sat down to eat, with the TV mumbling in the next room.

Suddenly Yanukovych's voice echoed loudly, wishing a happy New Year to the Ukrainian people. I jumped up from my chair, changed the channel, opened the champagne, and I had barely finished filling our glasses when the chimes of midnight sounded from the television. We clinked glasses, but without much enthusiasm. At least we had managed to buy a tree, though, and even to decorate it.

About half past midnight, Misha, Larisa, Natasha and I went out to the Maidan. The square was packed. There was music, and thousands of people celebrating the New Year, drinking champagne, taking pictures of each other in front of the tents and the barricades. We walked around for a while and then went home.

And suddenly, the feeling of celebration died once again. Usually at that sort of time, I get phone calls from twenty or thirty friends, or I call people myself to wish them a happy New Year, but last night there were very few calls or texts.

This morning I took Grandma Raya and Grandpa Yura to Borshchagovka, and Misha and Larisa to Nivki. I parked the car and we got ready to catch the train. Now for our holiday in Crimea. Last year, our holiday there was wonderful. But the weather was milder. This year, the forecast is gloomy. Grey skies, rain, temperatures around freezing. We have a sixteen-hour train ride ahead of us, in a sleeping compartment. We have packed a supply of food, with a bottle of wine for the adults and fruit juice for the kids. We are going to continue the New Year's celebration as we travel, just the five of us. Theo and Anton are already fighting over who gets to sleep in the top bunk. Gaby wants to sleep in the top bunk too. But there are only two top bunks, so one of the boys will have to give up his place.

Thursday 2 January

While we were on our way to Sevastopol, a torchlight procession took place in Kiev in honour of the 105th anniversary of Stepan Bandera's[10] birth. At the head of the procession marched Oleh Tyahnybok and other Svoboda leaders, among them the deputy, Andrey Ilyenko, son of the late film director Yuriy Ilyenko who made the film *Mazepa* at the request of Viktor Yushchenko, a fairly poor film with a strong anti-Russian slant. There were also two priests near the front, and a young girl carrying a portrait of Bandera, and behind them several thousand party members and supporters. They went up Mikhailovskaya Street, then Vladimirskaya Street, before taking Shevchenko Boulevard. As they were passing the five-star Premier Palace Hotel, one of the Svoboda deputies shouted through his megaphone something about the hotel and its guests.

Did he add anything else? I don't know, but soon after that several people ran from the procession to the hotel entrance and threw their torches into the lobby, near where hotel porters were standing guard. The porters managed to put out the flames, while the procession continued towards Bessarabskyi Square.

Klichko immediately stated that this march had nothing to do with the Maidan. And it's true. In fact, even better, it has nothing to do with Kiev. Kiev is a peaceful, tolerant city, which does not deserve to be shaken by processions and slogans yelled through megaphones. My morale is at rock bottom.

Friday 3 January

Crimea. Since this morning, the sky has been so low, it's practically leaning on the rooftops. The mountains are invisible. The rain falls heavily. We decided to go to Yalta in the hope that the weather might be better there. After an hour's journey in a minibus, we finally arrived at Yalta's bus station, where we took a trolleybus to the city centre. As soon as we left the station, we got caught in a traffic jam. I sat down in an empty seat, but just at that moment I saw an elderly and frail-looking old lady, so I offered her my seat. 'What excellent Russian you speak!' she said, wide-eyed. 'Are you from Russia?' No, I replied, I am from Kiev. 'Really?' she exclaimed, seeming genuinely surprised. 'And yet you speak Russian so well…' Probably because I was born in Leningrad, I suggested, hoping to provide an explanation she would find acceptable. 'Oh yes, probably,' she nodded. 'They speak such wonderful Russian in Petersburg!' She spent a good ten minutes trying to develop this theme, but from then on I merely listened and nodded. She spoke the same Russian as I did, it seemed to me, although it is true that the variant of Russian spoken in Crimea is generally different from that spoken in Kiev. The pronunciation is more emphatic here, each word clearly separated.

I ended up asking the conductor to open the front door. We got off and walked through the rain, passing two trolleybuses trapped in the interminable traffic jam. We eventually arrived at the docks. The boys wanted to practise their shooting. The manager of the shooting range offered them a wide variety of airguns, from revolvers to Kalashnikovs. Shooting with a compressed air rifle disguised as an assault rifle cost almost ten hryvnas, so I suggested to Anton and Theo that they opt for a less expensive model. The targets were crumpled beer cans, lined up on wooden shelves screwed to the wall opposite. Theo did quite well, but Anton only hit one beer can in ten attempts.

After walking to the Oreanda Hotel and back, we went into a restaurant, the Bakinsky Dvorik ('The Cosy Courtyard from Baku') and ate lunch. Theo ordered a Baku salad, which he spent a long time examining, describing each ingredient. Month by month, he seems ever more like a future chef. Last year, we came from Simeiz to Yalta to visit the Chekhov Museum in the white dacha. This time, because of the bad weather, we weren't in the mood for culture, so at 6 p.m. we took the last bus back to Foros.

Monday 6 January

Foros, Crimea. I called Natasha, in Katsiveli, this morning and told her we would arrive at lunchtime. Cool weather, almost no sunlight. We took the minibus and, by mistake, we got off too early, in Ponizovka. This provided the opportunity for a mile-long walk alongside the fence surrounding a vast unfinished complex from the Soviet era, which has belonged for many years now to the oligarch Ihor Kolomoyskyi, who lives in Switzerland. I wanted to show Liza and the children the Marine Hydrophysical Institute and its storm basin, but as we wanted to see a little more of Simeiz, I postponed that visit until another time.

Natasha had put on a great spread for our arrival. She had made borscht, salads, *kotlety*. I'd bought a small bottle of cognac on the way. We enjoyed a cheerful lunch.

Natasha's daughter and granddaughter ate with us. Natasha is readying herself for the next bathing season. She would like to come to an agreement with the Hydrophysical Institute about a place where hotel customers could park their cars.

When I explained to Theo and Anton that all these hotels belong to a cooperative of garages, they didn't believe me. So we went to the hotel next door, which is on four floors: the entire ground floor consists of parking spaces with real garage doors, from which hang Cooperative Parking signs. The kids burst out laughing.* Then we

---

* These hotels are legally not hotels but garages. In other words, they are registered with the Crimean authorities as garages. You will not find the word

went outside and, through the hedge, looked over at the unfinished chapel, the bottom part of which looks exactly like a garage. We didn't go inside the large church. That, too, is unfinished, and in truth does not look much like a garage. Presumably the president of the cooperative must have decided to build a chapel and a church here to ensure the support of the Orthodox Church, as all these constructions are illegal. But then, having agreed a non-aggression pact with the local authorities, perhaps he decided that the Church was no longer of any use to him, and so there was no need to finish building the chapel and its big sister. Better to build another four-storey garage for holidaymakers.

In Crimea, there are thousands of illegal hotels, maybe even tens of thousands. It makes no sense for the local government to fight this phenomenon. Instead of paying taxes, these hotels pay bribes to the Public Prosecutor, the police, the tax office and all the other local authorities. These judges and policemen can also turn up at any time to relax and eat dinner for free, or ask for a room for a few days for their friends or relatives. It's true that I myself spent a few days in this hotel last November, without paying a penny. But I had been invited here by one of the co-owners to work on a novel, which I did. In the spring – in April or May – I might come back for another week. There are lots of places to walk here, and the silence of Crimea is wonderfully conducive to working.

Having said goodbye to Natasha and her daughter, we walked to Simeiz. The path above the sea is barely more than a mile long, but it seemed endless because we kept stopping every five minutes to admire the waves or the mountains. There weren't any climbers this time at the foot of Mount Koshka. When we got to Simeiz itself, we gazed with sadness at the Villa Kseniya which, in 1990, used to be a cafe. We went there in October of that year, one year

---

'hotel' anywhere, which means they don't officially exist and nobody pays taxes on the profit received from guests staying there in the summer.

after our wedding. There was nothing in the shops, apart from choux buns at 15 kopecks each, tins of gobies in tomato sauce, and pearl barley. The cafe had no cakes or pastries. So we bought choux buns at one of the shops and, thus endowed, went and sat down at a table of the Villa Kseniya. Today this villa, like many of the other old buildings nearby, is in such a poor state that you feel it might collapse at any moment like a house of cards.

Then we went to Sova ('The Owl') where we wore ourselves out for an hour trying to finish a single game of Russian billiards. The balls simply refused to go down into the table's undersized pockets. Anton was the first to give up, sitting at a table with a glass of Pepsi and retreating into some kind of video game. Then Theo followed suit, and Liza and I were left alone to kill the time that we had already paid for. In the end, we didn't finish the game but simply decided not to play Russian billiards any more. The American version – pool – is much easier and more enjoyable.

When we came out, a cold and unpleasant wind was blowing through Simeiz. We took a minibus to the Sevastopol road and waited for another bus to Foros.

Wednesday 8 January

From the windows of one of our bedrooms, we have a clear view of the Black Sea, and from our kitchen we can see Foros Church perched on the mountain above the village. We can also see the mountain pass known as the Baidar Gates. Today, Theo, Anton and I climbed up there. First, we climbed up to the church, on fairly difficult and sometimes steep paths. Anton had insisted on taking a two-litre bottle of water and his tablet with him. Result: he had to carry a backpack. With this heavy weight on his shoulders, he tired more quickly than Theo and me, and we had to stop quite often.

At the summit, we spent a while on the little esplanade in front of the church, from where we could see not only Foros and the sea but also the neighbouring villages. I told Theo and Anton, once again, that Liza and I had come here in 1992, while they were preparing to reopen the church. In fact, it was already open, but still in the process of being restored. We had been welcomed by Father Pyotr. He offered to let me ring the bell that they had just hung in the bell tower. I pulled on the rope a few times, but after the first loud ring, the clapper came undone and fell to the ground with an almighty crash. 'Don't worry,' the priest said. 'We didn't attach it properly!' After that we went into his low little house, on the edge of the cliff, next to the church, and he placed a jar of jam on the table. The older members of his congregation, he explained, were constantly giving him jam and honey. And then, a few years later, we learned that Father Pyotr had been murdered. Murdered by a deserting soldier who had stayed with him. The murderer was found, and he said that he had killed the priest in order to steal from him, so he would have enough money to go far away. He didn't find any money in Pyotr's house, though. The priest didn't have any. All he had was a dozen jars of different kinds of jam.

There had not been anything to steal in the church either. The children and I went in. A couple, with a boy of five or six years old, turned round in our direction. We lit five altar candles for Ukraine, and paused a moment in front of the iconostasis, flanked by two decorated New Year trees.

When we got out, the couple and the little boy were getting into a car with Kiev plates. The man came up to me and said that we had met in the 1990s in the Petrovka book market. He had a little bookstall there. We chatted for five minutes, wished each other good luck, and then said goodbye.

Theo and Anton wanted to climb even higher, to the restaurant on the mountain pass. They serve huge, delicious *chebureki* there – those meat-filled pasties that are a speciality of the Crimean Tatars. We walked along a winding road and reached our goal in about half an hour, after several pauses to admire views of the Crimea. The restaurant was empty. They had Wi-Fi, so Anton immediately switched on his tablet and disappeared into another of his video games. We sat in the first room, near the window, and ordered three *chebureki* and Coca-Cola. That was how we celebrated the end of our holiday. Anton reminded me, once again, of my promise to buy him a more powerful computer when we got home.

Thursday 9 January

Sevastopol. The train is almost ready to depart. In front of the station: a Russian Unity Party minibus, with the Russian flag painted on its sides. I had never heard of this Ukrainian party, but there's nothing surprising about that. In Ukraine, there are 184 political parties registered with the Ministry of Justice. I can think of only one case where the ministry refused to register a party because of its name: the Putin Supporters Party. Strange that it should reject that but accept the Russian Unity Party! Perhaps because there is a big difference between 'being Russian' and 'being a Russian', although many Ukrainians don't seem to understand that. I am Russian myself, after all, an ethnically Russian citizen of Ukraine. But I am not 'a Russian', because I have nothing in common with Russia and its politics. I do not have Russian citizenship, and I do not want it. That is clearly why this party is described as the party of Ukrainian Russians. But then why do they have the Russian flag on their minibus? Because there is no flag for Ukrainian Russians?!

I bought the local papers at the station kiosk. We are swimming in darkness: bad news from Ukraine, all about the coming civil war. Calm down, citizens and journalists! There won't be a civil war! A civil war is carried out by one active part of the people against another active part of the people. One side desperately wants change, so desperately that their hands tremble; the other side desperately doesn't want these changes, and their hands tremble in a similar manner. Now tell me: where do you see two parts of the

Ukrainian people animated by the same level of desperate desire? I don't see them. I see the Berkut, I see the *titushky*, I see the sponsored *zelenka*,[*] I see a compliant legal system, but two halves of the same people in conflict with each other? No. Why does only one half of the people show, in its actions and words, its desire to live in a different way? Why does the second half remain mute and watch Ukrainian television? Why do the people in this second half agree, for the promise of 400 hryvnas, to attend rallies in support of the government, on buses chartered by the government, then complain, when they return home, that they were forced, as they were leaving the bus, to sign a receipt for 200 hryvnas, when they were given only 100, with the explanation that the other 100[†] was kept to pay 'for the journey'. That is what happened to *byudzhetniki* in the Zhytomyr region, and I doubt they were the only ones.

All over the country – in the Euromaidan, everywhere – the New Year holidays continue in spite of the situation. If everything happens in the Ukrainian way, then the political protests will not start up again until 20 January, after everyone has bathed, at Epiphany, in holes cut in the ice. This year, it's true, the air and water temperatures are milder. There is no ice. In fact, this year you could jump from the banks of the Dnieper straight into the river and immerse your entire body three times. God loves the Trinity. Last year, I bathed – with the Kapranov brothers, Lesya Ganzha, other writers, publishers and critics – on the banks of the Hidropark, opposite the Pechersk Lavra.

---

[*] *Zelenka* is a green dye, commonly used as an antiseptic in the countries of the former USSR. The ruling party supplies it to its activists so that they can spray protesters with it, as a way of humiliating them.

[†] The organisers of these political shuttle services would pocket 200 hryvnas from each participant, and then the juniors who were handing over the money would keep half of the remaining 200 for themselves.

Friday 10 January

The day had begun peacefully. When we got home, we drank tea to relax. I thought the country, still on holiday, would have a lie-in until 19 January, Epiphany in the Orthodox calendar, and that everyone would pray, take ice baths in lakes and rivers, say their usual interminable goodbyes to the New Year holidays, and only then throw themselves back into the fight. Revolutionaries, counter-revolutionaries, servants and guardians of the Yanukovych regime, and all the spectators to these battles, frightened by an uncertain future. These spectators form the overwhelming majority. They include in their ranks my Kiev publisher Petya Khazin and his wife, and my old friend Sasha Milovzorov, who, whenever we talk about the Maidan, exclaims: 'They've made the city a disgusting mess, those bastards!'

So anyway, the day had begun peacefully, but it ended in a mass battle with the Berkut near the Svyatoshino district court in Kiev, where some typical Ukrainian 'terrorists' were convicted. These people are currently known as Vasylkivite terrorists, because they are from the small town of Vasylkiv, about twenty-five miles from Kiev. For the crime of having incited a terrorist act – dismantling a statue of Lenin in another small town, Boryspil – they were sentenced to six years in jail. At the moment when the judge pronounced this sentence, the court was already surrounded by Svoboda supporters, as the defendants were members of that party. A bus full of *berkutovtsy* was parked nearby, in case any mass disorder arose. And it certainly did arise. First, the Svoboda supporters blocked the building's exits, preventing the judge from leaving. Then they began shaking the Berkut bus, before allowing its occupants to get out so that they could be made to walk through the corridor of shame. They filmed the *berkutovtsy* while this was happening, so that their colleagues and neighbours could identify them and put their names and addresses on the Internet.

How did Yuriy Lutsenko end up there? I haven't figured that out, but he is the one the *berkutovtsy* beat up. He has no connection with Svoboda, but he is linked to the Maidan. He was also one of the leaders of the Orange Revolution and Yushchenko's former Minister of Internal Affairs. According to the first version of the story I heard, he attempted to stop a possible conflict between Svoboda supporters and police special forces. The Ministry of Internal Affairs stated that he got into trouble because he was in a state of inebriation, a claim which he denied.

This evening, on TVI, the Batkivshchyna deputy Arsen Avakov attacked the Party of Regions deputy Oleg Kalashnikov, the latter famous for having punched a female journalist in the middle of Parliament two years ago because he didn't like the question that the journalist had asked. Had the presenter not held Avakov back as he was about to throw himself at Kalashnikov, we would have been spectators to another punch-up live on television.

Saturday 11 January

A cold day. On the attic floor, where the children's bedrooms are, the temperature is only 13°C. That is why the boys slept downstairs on the couch last night. Only Gabriela remained in her room upstairs, but she has an electric heater. Meanwhile, in Kharkiv, the Euromaidan Forum was taking place, chaired by the writer Serhiy Zhadan. When the Maidanistas gathered at the 'E' bookshop to discuss what strategy they should adopt now, scores of *titushky* swooped down on the store. They smashed the windows with clubs and released tear gas. They beat up the security guard who tried to stop them. He is in hospital, in danger of losing his sight.

Sunday 12 January

The Maidan's first *veche* of the year was held today, with 150,000 people taking part. The Automaidan's cars were lined up in the morning by European Square to carry out another motorised raid on Yanukovych's residence. The *veche* began with a prayer and speeches by priests from various denominations. Then Automaidan activists took to the stage and communicated their plans for the day. Speeches by politicians and activists were followed by the usual rock concert, featuring the groups Mad Heads, Mandry, Atmosfera and others.

Monday 13 January

This morning, all was strangely and surprisingly calm. And I was right to be suspicious of this peacefulness! At about 10 a.m., dozens of people wearing the same armband – yellow and blue with a red line in the middle, presumably to distinguish them from the Maidan activists, whose armbands are simply yellow and blue – attempted to bring down the barricades next to Bessarabskyi Market and the TsUM store. One of them, wielding a megaphone, declared that the Maidan was full of jobless and homeless people, and that Kievites were sick of this mess. These 'activists' were protected by a detachment of 'sportsmen', many of whom were members of provincial sports clubs. They didn't succeed in their mission, however, because several hundred Maidanistas arrived from Independence Square to help out the defenders of the barricades. After twenty minutes of yelling insults at each other, these representatives of Kievites left with their escort.

Tuesday 14 January

Last night, I went from my office to Shelkovichnaya Street through the Maidan barricades. I wanted to see Galya Listopad to explain to her that we will not be taking her bed for our country house.

On the stage in the Maidan, someone was talking about the anniversary of events in Vilnius. There were three or four hundred people listening. Next to the Hotel Ukraine, a Maidanista came out of a tent and looked like he was going to stop me, but I wasn't in the mood and I just kept walking. Sadovaya Street is still barred by buses and Kamaz construction trucks. Part of Shelkovichnaya Street is also sealed off by trucks. Berkut agents are posted there. Institutskaya Street is partly closed too, with only a narrow passage for cars, and a police officer directs traffic under the protection of the Berkut.

Snow fell, pretty and fluffy. No one was answering the phone. I stood outside the front door. Galya arrived soon afterwards. She told me she never took her phone with her, so she was only contactable early in the morning or late in the evening.

The renovation work in her apartment is nearly finished, and she has new Laura Ashley furniture. She is supposed to receive a sideboard and a bed tomorrow. At the moment, all her savings are going on Laura Ashley furniture, which she orders from a catalogue. In the apartment, I was greeted by her two cockatiels. I miss Kuzi, the male she had before and who is now dead.

I looked at the bed that I had finally decided not to take. I took a photograph of it. Galya tried once more to persuade me and I promised her I would give it further thought and ask Liza what she thinks. Suddenly Galya decided to give me her vacuum cleaner. She told me she was no longer going to vacuum in her apartment, instead making do with a mop. I took it in order not to upset her again. I get the feeling she is trying to clear even more space in her apartment, though it is hardly crowded even now. I didn't bother with the box it came in, as it was far too bulky. Galya found a bag that we managed to fit the vacuum cleaner inside, along with the pipe and the telescopic handle. I walked past the *berkutovtsy* and the student officers, carrying my vacuum cleaner. The bag was pink and the pipe stuck out of the top, so the police must have been intrigued, particularly as I was walking towards the Maidan. But nobody stopped me or took any notice, or asked me to show them what I was carrying. The snow continued to fall. On me, on the Maidan. They had lit makeshift braziers there, and people were standing around them to keep warm. Everything was the same as usual.

Wednesday 15 January

When I can't find the right words, my hand moves of its own accord towards books. Recently, this feeling of being lost for words comes over me more and more. Or life is becoming richer and stranger, or the words capable of describing it are shirking their responsibility. I am leaning towards the latter theory. People are using fewer and fewer words, and more and more interjections and gestures.

Yesterday evening, I finally bought Anton the computer I had promised him for New Year. The salespeople tried to flog me Microsoft Office with a one-year subscription. Is Bill Gates becoming a racketeer? A month ago, you could buy this software with a permanent subscription, even if you could only install it on one machine. I will look for another solution.

Outside, it's still freezing. In the Maidan, people are worried. The Internet is full of reports saying that the government is sending more and more soldiers and Berkut detachments to Kiev. Traffic police are terrorising members of the Automaidan. They have issued nine hundred tickets* confiscating driving licences for 'refusal to obey an order to stop'; all these tickets look as if they have been copied, and they are signed with an illegible name, so much so that it is difficult to work out which police officer is responsible. Mezhigorye is completely

---

* These tickets are police protocols with court decisions depriving the guilty ones of the right to drive for a period of one year.

surrounded by police special forces. Impossible to get there by car, as the road is blocked by buses and trucks. It is even impossible to walk around the neighbouring streets. The local farmers must have to struggle to find a way home among all the rows of police vehicles. They have to show papers proving that they really do live in the village. One old guy who didn't have his papers with him was hit with a truncheon for attempting to bypass this blockade so he could get home. Ukraine in the twenty-first century is like a return to the nineteenth century, before the abolition of serfdom.

In the evening, there are discussions on television about the interview given by Cardinal Lyubomyr Huzar from the Ukrainian Greek Catholic Church.[11] He said that when the government resorts to unjustified violence, the people have the right to resist them with the use of force. Political commentators working for Yanukovych and the Party of Regions are already outraged by this provocation. They are saying they should complain to the Pope about the cardinal and demand that the Ukrainian Greek Catholic Church stops getting involved in politics. One wonders why a priest from the Ukrainian Greek Catholic Church should not have the right to say Mass in the Maidan, while the Ukrainian Orthodox Church of the Moscow Patriarchate – the biggest Church in the country – is seemingly free to interfere in politics and to propagandise on behalf of Yanukovych and the Party of Regions during religious services whenever there is a parliamentary or presidential election. The Moscow Patriarchate represents millions of parishioners, the Greek Catholics just a few hundred thousand. Which one should be afraid of the other?

I found the interview in question, and here is the exact text:

There are situations where armed resistance may be permitted. When the government resorts to excessive violence, the people have the right to defend themselves with the use of force. Everyone has the right to defend himself. There is no need to write that in the constitution; it is the law of nature. I have the right to defend myself and my loved ones, as does every human being.

Thursday 16 January

It's raining.

Our old friend Yura Blashchuk, the financier, telephoned us. He and his wife Alisa have just flown in from Lithuania. They bought goat's cheese. Yura said he will drop by and give it to us at 11 a.m. Shame – I won't be there. I promised my parents I would drive them to their two banks so that they can withdraw their interest and renew their deposit.

We went to Legbank first. There, we got everything sorted fairly quickly. But at the second bank, where my father, I learned, has an account containing more than 100,000 hryvnas, there was a major inconvenience: the bank is not, for the moment, giving out cash. There were about thirty people standing in front of the counters, wondering what was happening or complaining about the situation. My father, who is eighty-seven, has got into the habit of putting his money in small and somewhat dubious banks that promise staggering interest rates, and then losing it all. This has already happened five times, but in spite of this he continues drawing his pension and depositing it in some new bank for which he's seen an ad in a free newspaper.

Friday 17 January

Yanukovych signed the laws voted for on a show of hands by the Party of Regions deputies. This circus of hands that nobody even counts is now 'legalised'. Happy days are coming, as happy as those in Moscow: no gatherings of more than three people in the street; SIM cards sold only upon presentation of ID, with registration in a special file, etc. Apart from these moronic laws, he also signed this year's budget. The army is only going to receive 40 per cent of its usual funding, but the police and judiciary will have 80 per cent more!

In Crimea, Russian patriots ransacked the monument to the Tatars of Crimea, victims of Stalin's deportations. Kharkiv is covered in snow, and on that snow, flying the Ukrainian flag, rides the Bikemaidan, made up of cycling enthusiasts.

I would like to get back to my Lithuanian novel. Ideas come to me, but I don't have the strength to concentrate. I always feel like going somewhere, and in order not to do this, I switch on the computer and check the latest news or I watch the *tableau vivant* of the Maidan or Hrushevskoho Street on the live streams on the Internet.

Sunday 19 January –
Day of Christ's baptism

Today, at 11 a.m., writers and publishers dived into the icy waters of the Dnieper, in our usual place – in the Hidropark, on the bank opposite the Pechersk Lavra. Shame I didn't manage to do it this year.

Hrushevskoho Street was also baptised. There were more than 10,000 protesters there, but also many more *berkutovtsy* and soldiers than there had been the day before. The police fired water cannons at protesters to chase them from the barricades. Outside, it is -7°C. But the Maidanistas, soaked to the skin, chanted: '*Vodokhreshcha! Vodokhreshcha!*' ('Baptism! Baptism!'). So that was 2014's version of Christ's baptism, with holy water delivered direct to the barricades.

Tuesday 21 January

The revolution continues, but I don't think it will last long. What is the point in fighting police if there is no single political direction for the protest movement, nor any common demands? It is really nothing but an outpouring of hatred for Yanukovych and the Party of Regions, for these corrupt dregs of society. But soon the state will strike back; there will be arrests and political prisoners. Their parents and children will form associations for the regime's victims. And the hatred will continue, as will the arbitrary arrests and the long prison sentences.

The opposition politicians have not come up with a joint proposal to offer the people, even if only for those ready to support them. Perhaps the politicians should have supported the people? But they couldn't, because they could never decide if they were making alliances or following the people's will. Everyone pursued their own ends. And those ends were not political but personal.

Wednesday 22 January

First deaths in Hrushevskoho Street. Why am I not surprised? Why does what seemed impossible or crazy before now seem logical and normal? We have all lost our minds.

I don't know what normal is. It is normal to despise a president who cannot write without making spelling mistakes, who knows nothing about anything, and who, apparently, never studied anywhere. Except perhaps during his two terms in prison as a young man. In other words, a president like Yanukovych cannot be normal. So it is normal to despise and reject him. The protests are the most direct form of this non-acceptance and non-love. That too is normal. When you attack the powers that be politically, they either react or ignore you. When you throw stones and Molotov cocktails at the powers that be – in other words, at the police – they reply with truncheons. Is that also normal? In Greece, yes. In Germany too. But in those countries, strangely enough, a person with a criminal record cannot become president!

The first victim of our internal intifada was called Serhiy Nigoyan, a twenty-year-old Armenian, a Ukrainian citizen, living in the Dnipropetrovsk region, who was seen reciting Shevchenko's poetry on the barricades. How can I keep working on a novel about Lithuania and Lithuanians when, five minutes from the office where I sit at this moment, in front of my computer, the police are waging war with the people, with radical romantics who could never, in any case, defeat the *berkutovtsy* – and, even if they did, what would we do afterwards? A godforsaken country, with smoke rising from it. Under that smoke, we are sharing power. Crooks and revolutionaries. In the future, the revolutionaries might become crooks. I doubt that the crooks will ever join with the revolutionaries.

The second victim of the day was a Belarusian citizen. And that's not all: in the Boryspil forest, where the activist Igor Lutsenko was taken and beaten, a corpse was discovered bearing traces of torture. It is probably the body of another activist abducted from hospital at the same time as Igor by unknown men in plain clothes. I wonder if the hospital has CCTV cameras. Is there a recording of this crime somewhere?

Thursday 23 January

The Maidan is still there. Presumably, Yanukovych developed a last-minute phobia of blood. All of Ukraine is watching a YouTube video at the moment, showing Kiev policemen, in Hrushevskoho Street, forcing a protester to strip off completely – a Cossack who, to judge from his appearance, is simply a member of one of the many clubs for history buffs. The minister Zakharchenko apologised for the policemen's behaviour and admitted that such acts are 'unacceptable in a civilised state'. He promised to punish the culprits. I expect he will punish them the way Yanukovych punished those involved in the violence against the students on 29 November. In other words, he will do nothing.

Sunday 26 January

Lazarevka. Sunlight on snow. And ideas of this kind: death does not love solitude. Only presidents are accustomed to it. People who, in their genes, guard the memory of serfdom, dream of becoming slave masters. Those who guard the memory of free men dream of liberty for all.

Our friend Vitya, the village's former telephone engineer, and Sasha, the former prison warden for the district, sold us fifty kilos of potatoes, at 5.70 hryvnas per kilo. I bought three extra buckets from the neighbour, Valya: those are for Petya Khazin. Coming back from the countryside, we stopped by at Grandma Raya's and then at Petya Khazin's, because his store of potatoes always dwindles too quickly.

Monday 27 January

-16°C, sunlight, silence. I drove the children to school, then went to see the revolution. I walked between the tents. Talked with revolutionaries. They were weary today. The air was thick with the smell of old campfires. Near the last metal barrel, with flames and smoke pouring from it, five or six people were standing around, motionless and strangely mute. There were probably no strangers among them. Everything has already been said. Conversation begins, out of habit, when someone approaches, a sympathiser or brother-in-Maidan.

Five or six vans selling coffee were lined up next to Bessarabskyi Square, a generator near each of them. Only one was open. I bought a coffee, then went to the Hotel Ukraine, where I did an interview with German television – on a small balcony, in the freezing air, the Maidan behind me. At 10 a.m., I met Swedish journalists and then went back with them to the barricades.

Half an hour later, having said my goodbyes, I went to visit the artists and other revolutionary *Kulturträger*. Among the hundreds of protesters' tents erected in the square, there is one that bears the name Mistetski Barbakan ('Artistic Barbican'). Though an active and fully integrated part of the Maidan, it has a life of its own. There is a permanent exhibition of revolutionary painting there, generally anarchistic and politicised, evoking the poster art of the 1918 Civil War. There are also book launches, concerts by singer-songwriters, readings by poets and writers. Revolution always gives impetus to the arts. It was the same in 1917 and after the October Revolution, and it is the same today. Handwritten or printed poems are stuck to fences and tents, in Russian and Ukrainian. Among the Euromaidan activists, there are writers, rock singers, even publishers. In between writing articles for websites and doing interviews, they help to build barricades. They are involved in the revolution despite being fully aware that, if they do not win the day, they are likely to face criminal charges and possibly prison sentences.

President Yanukovych, who, five weeks ago, 'did not notice' the actions and protests and refused to react to them, has suddenly published a decree quintupling the allowance for the National Taras Shevchenko Prize awarded to cultural contributors. He has also announced the establishment of nearly a thousand presidential grants for writers, poets, composers and other representatives of the artistic world. Someone should explain to him that no well-known painter or writer would want to give him their support, just as no pop star or rock singer would agree, even for a huge fee, to play at a rally organised by the government.

Art in Ukraine has long been detached from political power – ever since the beginning of the independence movement, in 1991. The Ministry of Culture still exists, in spite of this. In 2004, at the time of the Orange Revolution – a genuinely peaceful revolution, that one – some writer colleagues and I organised three weeks of political debates between representatives of the two sides in a large bookshop – Naukova Dumka ('Scientific Thought') – on European Square. People came into the shop to warm up, because at the time (like today, in fact) it was between -15 and -20°C outside. That bookshop is closed now, and will be for the duration of the revolution. The first line of barricades is right next to it, and beyond that are parked vehicles belonging to the police and the special forces, equipped with shields and guns for dispersing protesters. The proverb, which exists in many languages – *When the cannons are heard, the muses are silent* – proves only partly true in Kiev. The cannons are heard every night in just one place in the city centre: in Hrushevskoho Street, the street that leads to the government and Parliament buildings. Each night there are clashes there between activists and special forces. Both sides throw Molotov cocktails, but the special forces also have rifles loaded with rubber bullets, grenades that can cause injuries, and a host of other equipment. And not only are there special forces, there are also secret forces who act against the protesters: many people have been injured by metal bullets, and several killed by weapons of war that the special forces, theoretically, do not possess. Dozens of activists and protesters have been abducted at night by men in plain clothes driving vehicles with false number plates. Many of these kidnapped people have then turned up in police stations, but some have never been found. One of them, identified as activist Yuriy Verbitsky, was discovered in the forest near Kiev, dead, his body showing signs of physical abuse.

Friday 31 January

-23°C this morning. No school because of the cold, but I had to go to the studios of Channel 1+1 for the news programme. Bags under my eyes, feeling like I'd been squished beneath a steam-roller. Still half asleep, I made a few confused remarks about the political situation and then went home.

Yesterday's main news was that Dmytro Bulatov, the leader of Automaidan, has been found – in a terrible state, but alive. He was abducted by unknown men on 22 January, and they tortured him for a long time in an attempt to make him answer this question: who is funding Automaidan? He never saw his torturers; he only heard them. On the night of the 22nd, he was hit on the head before being taken away. He was released in the Boryspil district, thrown from a car near a village. The last time, it was Yuriy Verbitsky who was released in this way: not near a village, but in the forest, and he was dead. The same people.

Yanukovych hides from the country's eyes by taking sick leave. His other servants of the people are simply sick.

Theo, who had received 3,000 hryvnas for his birthday, gave us 1,000 back. He said 2,000 was enough. Thank you, Theo. Tomorrow he will use the 2,000 to pay for paintball and pizza. Theo and Anton have also agreed to save the money we would have spent on a restaurant. Instead, I will cook noodles in Thai sauce with chicken for dinner.

Monday 3 February

A very cold and sunny day. On Saturday, I took Theo, Anton and eight other children to the party in the Hidropark, at the Paintball Planet club. The plastic bullets filled with red paint froze and exploded inside the gun barrels, but the kids waged war for almost two hours, with breaks to clean the guns.

On Sunday, Liza and I went to the Maidan, taking five kilos of buckwheat *kasha*. We were preparing a grown-up celebration of Theo's birthday when we learned that Natasha Kolomoytseva was ill – heart problems. She had called for an ambulance and been taken straight to the hospital. Then Ira Khazina called to say she probably wouldn't be able to come, because she had bronchitis, and that Petya would stay to look after her. So that is how we came to celebrate the event with three guests instead of six. The beef with rosemary was perfect. We drank tea and ate cake in front of the fire. It all ended quite early, about 8.30 p.m. But it was a nice evening.

And today, at eleven in the morning, I went to the Vidrodzhenie ('Renaissance') Foundation, where a board meeting was being held for a humanitarian initiative providing medical assistance for victims of the regime. There are three writers on the supervisory board: Serhiy Zhadan, Oksana Zabuzhko and myself. The fourth member will be the former Health Minister, Vasil Kniazevich. Zabuzhko attended the meeting only virtually, by telephone. She said that current events were merely the beginning of a third world war, that postmodernism's time was over, etc. The foundation director, Yevgeniy Bystritsky, gave us a copy of a strange and very aggressive speech by Igor Lutsenko, the Maidan activist: *'Those who spilled blood'* – undoubtedly an allusion to Pravy Sektor, the far-right nationalist party – *'have the right to govern the country. Everyone fight until the final victory!!!'* and so on, all in the same belligerent style. In other words: the war continues.

The Kapranov brothers were barely allowed to mount the stage in the Maidan to announce the decision to organise a forum. They were bewildered and upset. Revolutionaries are becoming superfluous to this revolution. Complete unknowns decide who is allowed to speak onstage, and who should be prevented.

Tuesday 4 February

The weather has warmed up considerably: -10°C. I have been to the central post office to send letters by registered post. Just in front of the freight office, about fifteen warmly dressed Maidanistas were putting up a new tent.

A veil of mist hangs above the Maidan today, as over the Sri Lankan jungle in the mornings. The sun is blinding, and it is not yet at its zenith. There are few people around.

Last night, our neighbours started a wave of panic. They telephoned me several times because a big guy, about six foot two, has been standing at the entrance to the staircase for the past three days. He seems to be watching out for someone, observing. I noticed him too, as I was going through the lobby, but at that time – about six in the evening – he was outside, in front of the building. Presumably he went indoors to get out of the cold. When I went out later in the evening to attend a meeting with Yuriy Makarov in the 'E' bookshop, he was no longer there.

This morning, I had a long conversation in the courtyard with the notary on the ground floor. He told me that there used to be another, smaller man who stood guard there all the time. Obviously in the line of duty. Apparently it's because of the office on the first floor which one of the Maidan leaders, Yegor Sobolev, has visited several times. The notary and I calmly examined the problem, but we didn't find a solution. We wished each other a good day and went our separate ways. At the Bacchus restaurant, I met with the owner, the former banker Sasha Savchenko, who is also a friend of mine. He suggested I gather a group of intellectuals in his restaurant once a month to chat about the situation, accompanied by good wine and a light snack.

On the way home, at the steps on Franko Street, I met up with Anton and Tanya. Anton tried to convince me to let him off going to the music school today. After a brief conversation, I agreed. He was incredibly happy, and promised me he would do his Ukrainian homework.

Meanwhile, the Crimean Parliament discussed the peninsula's separation from Ukraine and its conversion into an autonomous region of Russia. Vadim Titushko suddenly announced that he supported the Maidan, and that, had he not been under house arrest, he would go to Kiev to chop wood for the Maidanistas' camping stoves. Tymoshenko, from her hospital bed, declared that she was against a return to the 2004 constitution. This is understandable: she wants to become president with full powers.

Wednesday 5 February

The temperature is up to -2°C. One of my editors has confirmed that I will be doing a tour of universities in western Ukraine on 12 and 13 February: Rivne, Ostroh, Khmelnytskyi. This morning, I listened to the news on the radio while I was waiting for the car's engine to warm up. I had the impression that part of the news was repeated every day, that there must be a recording on file: 'Ania, how are things in the Maidan?' 'Everything is calm in the Maidan. There aren't many people here. People woke up, they sang the Ukrainian anthem. The priests recited the morning prayer for the country. The people are pulling themselves together. The protesters have begun to restore order to the square.'

There are a few themes that have recurred continually since the Orange Revolution, making the situation similar to the beginning of a classic chess match: instead of e2–e4, Kiev descends into turmoil, the east announces either the organisation of an armed resistance or the formation of an autonomous republic, Crimea asks Russia to send troops in and annex the peninsula. Then the civil servants and the pro-government politicians begin to blow on their compatriots in an attempt to put out, as quickly as possible, their obvious stupidity.

Yesterday, Parliament announced an open forum day. Everyone was given the chance to speak. Or, in other words, no one listened. Yanukovych has gone into hiding again and is remaining silent while he waits to take the presidential aeroplane to Sochi, for an Olympic meeting with Putin. Hanna Herman, the president's adviser, stated that the president would not make any decision over the resolution of the crisis before discussing it with his Russian counterpart. But of course not! What could he possibly do without Putin? Who could he possibly take advice from in Ukraine? There is no one here who can match the Russian president when it comes to strategic thinking.

Unpleasant rumours are growing around some of the leaders of the protest movement. One of them, Oleksandr Danilyuk, fearful of being arrested, illegally crossed the border and reappeared in London. I didn't realise we shared a border with Great Britain. He said he had walked, in bitterly cold conditions, while a snowstorm raged on the plain. But the only plain in Ukraine is on the border with Russia. I somehow doubt he went that way. Dmytro Bulatov was officially transported to Lithuania for treatment following his abduction. Apparently, some people believe the government's claims that he wasn't really kidnapped by Russian special forces or any other group known for their brutality, and that his kidnapping was staged to stir up the situation. After a similar abduction, Igor Lutsenko appeared terribly bruised and dejected, even though he had only been beaten for one day. Yuriy Verbitsky died from his ordeal. Tatyana Chornovol, the victim of violence in the Boryspil district, was bedridden for two weeks, her face so swollen she was barely recognisable. Bulatov was held for eight days. They say if he had been tortured continually for that long, he would not have survived.

Thursday 6 February

Yesterday: a brief meeting with a Norwegian photographer, Tom Kristensen, in the Dnipro Hotel. The main entrance is shut off and deep in shadow, as if the place were closed. But it is definitely open, and you have to enter through the London Pub to the left. Inside, there's a little sentry box with a window, manned by a black employee. There's also a security guard sitting on a stool close by. The bar actually functions.

Kristensen has been to Berdychiv and other towns. He wanted to talk about an interview I gave, published in a Norwegian newspaper, in which I said that Ukraine urgently needed psychologists because there were, at the moment, two groups of citizens in the country suffering from psychic trauma: those traumatised since childhood, particularly in the east of the country, and those in the centre and the west, of perfectly sound mind at the beginning of the protest movement but who, their cries of protest having gone unheard, have also been traumatised, and have been transformed from romantics into radicals.

The four hours I spent in the evening at the Hotel Ukraine's sauna passed like a party, ephemeral but joyous. Dan Yanevsky showed up dressed like a dandy in hat and coat, twirling a walking stick with a shiny gold head. The sports journalist Dima Kharitonov arrived after everyone else. The publisher Krasovitsky advised me to leave Kiev with my family before Friday, as he fears that blood will be spilled.

After the sauna, we crossed the Maidan towards the Kozatskiy

Hotel, where Dima's car was parked. On Institutskaya Street, a line of young men in helmets was forming, waving UDAR and other flags. To the left of the Independence monument – at the foot of that girl perched on a stick, as it's known – eight people were playing giant chess. On the other side of the Maidan, we passed a small group of short-haired, nervous-looking youths, aged about sixteen. They were speaking Russian, and the acronym 'SS' kept coming up in their conversation. Near a tent, in front of an extinguished brazier, stood a well-dressed, elderly woman, with a vacant look in her eyes. She was staring into space, as if she had no idea where she was, as if she had lost her memory.

This morning, the radio announced that Yanukovych had offered Poroshenko the position of head of the NBU, Ukraine's national bank. If he accepts, there is the possibility that a coalition government will be formed. 'Yanukovych is screwed,' Dan said in the sauna.

During the night, I noticed on Facebook that a woman with a Lithuanian name had been looking at my old photographs. I clicked to see what she'd been interested in, and saw the picture of Serhiy Nigoyan, when he was still alive. That gave me a shock. I had taken his photograph in December in the Maidan, a month or so before his death, a big smile on his bearded face, a placard in his hand: *God speaks through the voice of the people.*

A letter from Tymoshenko was published yesterday, a letter which – according to rumour – has stirred up conflict in the opposition, dividing it into two camps and causing Yatsenyuk to lose his grip on the leadership of Batkivshchyna. What Tymoshenko fears is an agreement with Yanukovych and a coalition government, which would mean that the opposition politicians had forgotten she was still being held in her hospital prison.

Today, a box that supposedly contained medicine exploded in the Trade Unions building. A volunteer lost his hand. The police sealed off the place. Their version is that home-made bombs were being manufactured inside the building and that one of them must have gone off prematurely.

Yesterday, a first wedding was celebrated in the Maidan! A story worthy of a romance novel: injured during a protest march, young Yulia, from Rovno, went to the infirmary. Bogdan, a volunteer from the Zhytomyr region, bandaged her hand. After that, Yulia ended up volunteering at the Maidan's infirmary too. And yesterday, in Kiev's city hall, where the two of them have lived since the day the building was seized by revolutionaries, everything was made spick and span and the red carpet was rolled out for the young couple. The wedding ceremony was conducted by two priests who blessed the union and wished the newly-weds happiness and courage in their struggle for Ukraine. Some deputies turned up, but only from the Svoboda Party. The party's leader, Oleh Tyahnybok, gave the couple a bouquet of white roses and a set of bedlinen. At the end of the ceremony, Yulia and Bogdan went to the barricades together.

Last night, thirty or forty people in balaclavas smashed the windows of two restaurants, including the O'Panas in Shevchenko Park. The *titushky* are suspected. Strange that a photographer from the newspaper *Segodnia* ('Today') should happen to be at the scene of the crime at three in the morning! Are vandals inviting journalists to come with them nowadays?

Friday 7 February

I went to my office this morning. As I was entering the building, I noticed a procession of protesters with Batkivshchyna flags marching off towards the Golden Gate. Now I understand why so many policemen were roaming the streets in the centre of town. The day before yesterday, the Party of Regions deputy Oleg Tsarov claimed that a commando unit of American parachutists had landed in western Ukraine. He was demanding that Russian army tanks be sent in. I can already see them crossing the whole country, all the way to the western border, searching for American soldiers, and then going home and apologising to us for the disturbance!

No reassuring news. Yanukovych flew out to Sochi for the Olympics. On the Net, you can hear a personal conversation between Victoria Nuland, the American Assistant Secretary of State for European affairs, and Geoffrey Pyatt, the US ambassador to Ukraine, in which the former says 'Fuck the EU' for its weakness regarding Ukraine. Yesterday, the *titushky* were standing outside the Lithuanian embassy to protest against European involvement in Ukraine.

In Lviv today – forty days after the terrorist attacks in Volgograd, Russia – Maidan activists honoured the memories of victims of the two bombs that exploded in a trolleybus and in the central station. A Mass was held on the stage in the local Maidan. The city's inhabitants lit altar candles and decorated the stage with black mourning crepe.

Sunday 9 February

Lazarevka. Two nights in the countryside. Traditional forms of protest in eastern Ukraine: miners refusing to come up to the surface, or banging on their helmets in front of the mines management and the local authorities. Then they march on Kiev, banging their helmets on the steps of Parliament and the Cabinet building. The government only knows what Ukraine is from an eastern perspective. And that is why it doesn't know how to combat the Maidan. Even Hanna Herman, the Galician deputy, despite being a defector from the western part of the country, cannot help Yanukovych understand because she has never been a representative of the western Ukrainian or pro-Ukrainian political mentality. The current government has no advisers, hence this stalemate.

The government is used to seeing in western Ukrainian protest movements a sort of theatrical-religious show without any political consequences for Kiev. Until now, it has not really had to worry about protests except for those in its own territory, as lifestyle determines style of protest. In other words, demonstrations in the east can be much more violent and chaotic than those in the west. Given the apolitical nature of eastern Ukrainian society, the demands of local movements can only be material or, in rare cases, related to the shameless behaviour of representatives of the legal system or other state powers.

After the online publication of photographs showing Berkut agents throwing Molotov cocktails at protesters, the Ministry of

Internal Affairs made an official declaration that Molotov cocktails no longer constituted part of the police's weaponry, and that those responsible would be held accountable.

Tuesday 11 February

I spend the morning writing an article in the apartment. After lunch, I go to Ukraine House, where there is supposed to be a round table involving my fellow writer Andrukhovych. As I am going in, the Maidan security staff ask me for my pass. I say I don't have one. They ask to see any other sort of ID. I take out a copy of one of my books and show them my photograph on the back cover. They let me in.

As I sit down to wait for the round table to begin, I receive a call from Gaby: 'Tanya left, so I'm on my own, and there are three guys dressed in black hanging around in front of the door. I'm scared. What should I do?' If they ring the doorbell, don't answer the door, I tell her. Lenya, the antiquarian, is sitting next to me. He sees the worried look on my face and asks me what's wrong. I tell him. So he hails Sergey, the head of Automaidan security. 'We have to go!' he says. We leave, getting in a taxi driven by his friend Andrey. On the way, another phone call from Gaby: 'They rang the doorbell, but I didn't answer!' Don't open the door for anyone, I tell her; we'll be there soon. We get stuck in a traffic jam, but finally we arrive. We go through the courtyard. Sergey puts on gloves and says he's going in alone. He suggests I stay behind in the car. Asks me to call Gaby so she will open the door to him. He will introduce himself as Karl.

After ten minutes, he still hasn't returned. I begin to feel nervous. I suggest to Andrey that we go into the building. I see men on the second floor, from behind. We go back to the courtyard.

Sergey appears under the archway. He explains to us that one of the men is a cop, and the other two 'normal guys'. They claimed they were waiting for the tenants in apartment number 8 and they talked about reinforced glass windows. It all sounds like bullshit to me: apartment number 8 is vacant. Sergey took pictures of them and got their mobile phone numbers. Everything is under control. They won't do anything now. We can leave.

We go back to Ukraine House. The round table isn't over. There are about thirty people listening to the speakers, and many more coming and going in the building, carrying baseball bats, wearing helmets and bulletproof vests. Volunteer doctors from the Maidan walk past them. I feel worried. I can't stay sitting down. I end up leaving. I go to my office to pick up my computer and head home. This time, the stairwell is empty. All is calm, silent.

In the evening, Gaby tells Liza what happened. Liza isn't happy. 'Stop playing at James Bond!' she says. I don't think she realises the gravity of the situation.

Thursday 13 February

Ostroh. Yesterday, after seven hours in a bus, I finally reached Rivne. We stopped at bus stations in different district centres and in Zhytomyr. A *belyash** vendor got on the bus, then a woman in her fifties, carrying a black plastic bag. She asked people to put money in the bag so she could afford to have an operation. Around me, I heard strange phone conversations. A respectably dressed man said he was going to Lviv, via Rivne. By bus, then train, and once he got to Rivne he would book a plane ticket to Lviv for someone, even though Warsaw would have been better, because the person had to go on to Katowice. The driver, who had been speaking Russian in Kiev and until we entered Zhytomyr, now switched to Ukrainian.[12]

At the station in Rivne, Viktoria and Mark were waiting for me: two young people, slightly Rasta. They look after an association called Literature V, arranging meetings with writers, for which they sell tickets. They make enough money to live, but obviously not in any great luxury. Everything was perfectly organised, though, both at the university and then at Knizhny Supermarket.[†] I slept to my heart's content in an empty apartment next to the bus station that Viktoria and Mark had rented for two nights. And this morning, having got to Ostroh more quickly than I expected, I took a walk around the northern part of the town. The streets were calm, almost deserted, with lots of dogs in kennels.

---

* Meat pasty of Tatar origin.

† Chain of bookshops whose name translates as 'Book Supermarket'.

Chaos still reigns throughout the country. The Party of Regions is loudly demanding federalisation; they would like to remain in power in their fiefdoms, the way the leaders of the Communist Party in each republic remained in power after the USSR collapsed. But the tension in Kiev is building. Here, in Ostroh, 175 miles from the capital, all is silent and calm. There are faded, crumbling posters on lamp posts and telegraph poles saying: *Everyone to Kiev! Let's support the Maidan.*

Yesterday, after the meeting in the bookshop, I was approached by Aleksandr Osovets, an 'Aspenite'.* We drank tea together. He was wondering what could be done locally to enliven and support public life. We talked about a possible essay competition, open to young people, on the theme 'The future belongs to us', with the idea of bringing together the finalists in Rivne, organising a debate and attempting to create a club, with a Facebook page and future meetings.

---

* A participant in the Aspen seminars organised in Ukraine. These seminars began a few years ago in Aspen, USA. Before each meeting, the participants read historical and philosophical texts – from ancient Greece to the contemporary era – then discuss them in the seminar.

Saturday 15 February

At one in the morning, at Khmelnytskyi station, I caught a train from Ivano-Frankivsk, heading to Kiev. I slept fully dressed on the top bunk and arrived, on time, at 6.12 a.m. By seven, I was home. I lay down and slept for a couple of hours. Ignoring my tiredness and headache after a too-brief and agitated sleep, I decided we should go to the countryside. Gaby stayed in Kiev with a friend – an experiment – while Bogdan, a friend from Anton's class, came with us.

That evening, the first national television channel showed an interview given by Yanukovych to a journalist who had been very well known during the Soviet era, Vitaliy Korotich. Absolutely dreadful. Korotich, with his bags under his eyes, looked old and weary. Yanukovych appeared to be wearing a mask, only the mouth moving slightly, the movements never coinciding with the words we heard. He talked nonsense. I switched off.

Today, Klichko is supposed to appear in Poltava. The police and the fire brigade have already surrounded the building where the event is due to take place and they are not letting anyone in. They have cut the power and announced a bomb alert.

In Kiev, the opposition has agreed to clear out part of Hrushevskoho Street and to evacuate the city hall. But the opposition is one thing; the protesters are quite another. The Maidanistas have condemned the opposition's promises. No one has any intention of leaving Ukraine House, the October Palace or the Trade Unions building. Again, there are rumours of troops converging on Kiev, rumours that a new operation against the protesters will be mounted on Monday. A Molotov cocktail was thrown at Hanna Herman's parents' house, in the Lviv region. The house did not burn down, at least not completely.

The library in the Maidan has begun donating books to village libraries. Mila Ivantsova, Galya Vdovichenko and other writers are taking care of this. In some villages, the authorities have forbidden libraries to accept books with the stamp 'Maidan Library' and declared that if any of their librarians do take these books, either they will be forced to tear out the pages bearing this stamp or they will be fired.

To begin with, Leonid Kozhara, the Foreign Minister, criticised the Russian diplomat who claimed that Ukraine was already, de facto, federalised, but yesterday Yanukovych announced that he would have to re-examine the possibility of a federalisation.

The veterans of the Afghanistan war supported Euromaidan, then a group of them declared an armistice and left, upset that the masters of the barricades on Hrushevskoho Street did not listen to their professional opinions about combat. Last night, presumably in an attempt to persuade the remaining 'Afghans' to leave the centre of Kiev, Yanukovych established a medal for the '25th anniversary of the withdrawal of Soviet troops from Afghanistan'.

In Simferopol, an American named Jeffrey Lubbi was beaten up simply because one of his Ukrainian friends, when asked what he thought of the Maidan, replied that he fully supported the protest movement.

Near Kiev, farmers discovered the corpse of a man in a field, dressed like a Maidanista with a blue-and-yellow ribbon in his jacket, his face disfigured.

Sunday 16 February

Lazarevka. A nice, peaceful morning. On the ground outside the living-room window are the sides of an old kitchen cupboard that we replaced in the autumn. Anton, Bogdan and Theo attempted to use them to make a kennel for Ryzhik, a stray dog from the village who apparently adopted us yesterday evening and imagines, poor thing, that he has found someone to look after him.

Last night, in Kiev, the city hall was slowly evacuated, with the Maidanistas moving their things out. But there was a commotion on Hrushevskoho Street. The radicals agreed to clear a passage for vehicles. Two bulldozers arrived, sent by the government. While this was happening, trucks and cars with trailers were bringing the Hrushevskyites sand and lime to reinforce the barricades (which are beginning to melt, now that the weather is improving). The traffic police attempted to stop them as they drew near the centre, but the vehicles managed to reach their destination. At the same time, a checkpoint was set up, enabling traffic to be regulated.

Monday 17 February

Yesterday, Liza and I ate breakfast at the Maystruks', leaving the children enough food to make their own breakfast in the kitchen. And today we drove the Maystruks' son Vovchik to Kiev. We had just arrived and unloaded the car when the people below us knocked at the door and told us that there had been loud noises coming from the apartment until three in the morning: Gaby and her friends had thrown a party. The experiment is a failure.

While we were driving from Zhytomyr towards Kiev, we saw an Automaidan procession speeding past in the opposite direction: in front, a powerful three-wheeled motorbike with a black-and-red flag. Behind, a dozen people carriers and saloon cars, some of them dented, with mangled bumpers and crumpled sides. Following them were five or six traffic police cars. Soon after that, we passed a police patrol that had stopped several Automaidan vehicles. Closer to Kiev, the same story again. The police are attempting to chop up the Automaidan into little groups.

In the afternoon, Piatras and I took the car to go and see Yura and Alisa. All over the city, and along the roads to Kontsa-Zaspa and Obukhov – every five hundred yards, by the roadside – there were two or three police cars. The officers were stopping all cars flying Ukrainian flags. So now the national flag has become a sign of anti-government activity!

Today, as I learned when I arrived in Lisnyki at Yura and Alisa's place, we were celebrating the national holiday of Lithuania. We stayed until 8.30 p.m., drinking wine and playing pool.

Then I received a call (the second) from Ira, who asked me if I could help them obtain multiple-entry Lithuanian visas, because they had decided to celebrate 8 March in Lithuania! It is clear that they would like to flee the country in these troubled times and that they are trying everything possible to get Schengen visas.

The return of the city hall to the authorities has caused a great deal of discontent. After it occurred, a group of people in balaclavas, armed with clubs, went up to the fifth floor and trashed the offices. We still do not know if they were agitators or if they really were members of the paramilitary organisation Patriots of Ukraine wishing to avenge their comrades from Vasilkov who were sentenced to prison.

According to the newspapers, Ukrainian oligarchs have not had access to foreign borrowing for the past two months now. I doubt that.

On Hrushevskoho Street, the barricades have melted. Many members of the self-defence groups no longer hide their faces; they walk around in helmets, smiling, once again allowing bystanders to take their photos. A young woman with her six-year-old son came to look at the blackened street. The passage, the clearing of which marked an important step in unblocking the street, is very narrow, indistinct, almost non-existent. And utterly meaningless because, beyond there, in any case, stretch the cordons of Berkut agents – so much so that no traffic can possibly flow through. Everywhere you see piggy banks bearing the words: *Help for victims*. Behind Ukraine House, in the building's courtyard, you can hear the sound of sticks colliding: a detachment of self-defence groups in training.

Tuesday 18 February

Galya Listopad came last night with leaflets listing the companies and goods with links to the Party of Regions. We finished
off the chicken cooked in Lazarevka. Liza claimed to be worried
for the employees of the Kievkhleb – the large industrial bakery
in Kiev – if we boycott their bread. Then Galya had a go at Leonid
Novokhatko for his letter against the Ukrainian Greek Catholic
Church. This time, I stepped in to defend the Minister of Culture,
reminding her that the letter had been signed by Tymofiy Kokhan,
the deputy minister, while Novokhatko was in Austria. We ended
the discussion in a more or less peaceful way, agreeing that I
would stop by the following week with Theo to pick up the famous
bed from her apartment. We will dismantle it, attach it to the roof
rack and attempt to transport it to Lazarevka. This was yesterday,
but because of today's events, I have the impression that all that
happened a long, long time ago.

This morning, I phoned the Brusilov police station to tell them
that a vandal had destroyed the gates in my driveway. I said: 'Is
this the police station?' Politely and hastily they replied: 'Yes, I'm
sorry, but we're watching the assembly debate!' And then they
hung up. It didn't even cross their mind to wonder if someone
might be asking for help or reporting a crime.

I went for a walk in the Maidan, watching the smoke rise from
tyres that were once again on fire. I was waiting for a call from Marc
Sagnol, who was supposed to have already arrived, but my phone
remained silent. Marc is an old friend who was the director of the

French Institute in Kiev fifteen years ago. He was supposed to spend the night at our house. I kept going until I reached Petya's apartment, and from there, I called him myself. He was still at the airport.

Beginning early in the morning, there was a rally around the Rada – Ukraine's parliament – to demand a return to the 2004 constitution. Violence soon broke out, and the Berkut sent in the *titushky*. And then, about two o'clock, the situation suddenly worsened. Activists invaded the Party of Regions headquarters and set fire to it. The Berkut threw grenades and fired rubber bullets, from the ground and from the rooftops. The self-defence groups seized the Officers' House, and the dead and the wounded were sent there. By four in the afternoon, there were already three dead, a priest from the Kiev Patriarchate reading them their last rites.

Another priest, Alexander, was caught by the *titushky* and beaten up. They broke his arm. The clashes spread. On the news, it said negotiations had taken place between unknown parties in the president's office, and at the same time that the president had done a runner, taking off in an aeroplane from Boryspil airport.

The *berkutovtsy* attacked the barricades at the top of the Maidan, and almost five thousand people retreated into the square. The *veveshniki* had encircled Ukraine House.

What about the October Palace? Leaving the Rada, the opposition deputies walked towards the Maidan. And the Trade Unions building? It is possible that it will all be over by this evening...No, it can't be over. There might be a break in the action, but Ukraine cannot be reduced to the Kiev Maidan. What will happen next? The dissolution of Parliament, the announcement of new elections in six months, the lifting of parliamentary immunity for opposition deputies and their arrests? This country has never had such a stupid president before, capable of radicalising one of the most tolerant populations in the world!

While I was walking down Khreshchatyk Street, I passed other people looking preoccupied, mobile phones glued to their ears. A guy next to me: 'What, for 250 hryvnas? You'd support those queers for 250 hryvnas?! Well, all right. Call me as soon as you're free!' A woman on Proreznaya Street: 'What? Who got beaten up? Oh, communists? Well, that's good!'

I am now in an aeroplane, on my way to Bavaria, where I will deliver a talk on the situation in Ukraine. Nataliya Gumenyuk, from the Internet channel Hromadske.tv, was supposed to accompany me. She hasn't. And she was right. Better to stay in Kiev and report on events as they unfold. When I'd called Liza, she had been getting ready to leave her office. All British Council staff were being sent home. Before take-off, I called Gaby and Theo to give them instructions: don't open the door, don't go out in the street, etc. But there was actually some good news on Hromadske. tv today: Zhako the parrot can now sing the national anthem and respond to the words, 'Glory to Ukraine!' As for me, I took off.

Yesterday, Liza suggested for the first time that we might have need of our house in Whitstable, in England. The tenants are leaving in March. Our estate agent is ready to find new ones. Let him look, I replied. 'Yes, there are people we can stay with if we need to,' Liza concluded.

Valera Mikhailov called to ask me to take part in a Shevchenko evening on the 28th. I promised to be there. And my old schoolteacher Oleg Bobrov asked me to be in Obolon on 3 March.

When I checked the newsfeed in Boryspil earlier, I saw the interview with the novelist Miroslav Dochinets, saying that he was willing to accept the Shevchenko Prize from Yanukovych because the prize bears Shevchenko's name, not the president's, and that he had listened to the opinions of his readers, who had encouraged him to accept the money. And that he would find a way to spend it in a useful way, because that money was not Yanukovych's but the state's.

Wednesday 19 February

In Kiev, they are counting the dead, the wounded and the disappeared. Among the latter: Stepan Khmara, a former dissident who
spent many years in a Gulag for anti-Soviet activities. He left his
house to go to the Maidan, and he vanished. This night of warfare
has transformed the city centre to ruins.

Strangely, during these three months, the smoke from the
protests has never reached our house. The wind always takes
it towards the government district, towards Parliament and the
Cabinet building. And yesterday, late afternoon, this smoke gave
way to flames: the big Trades Union building was burning, and still
is, in Kiev's central square, a building constructed in the Soviet era
to host the central committee of all the unions. For two months, it
had been occupied by protesters. They had installed a hospital to
treat the wounded, and several thousand people, come from other
regions to protest, have spent the night there. Yesterday, it was
seized by the *berkutovtsy*, and soon afterwards the building was on
fire. An opposition deputy, Sergei Sobolev, announced that more
than a hundred seriously injured protesters had been staying
there, and that only half of them had been evacuated before the
fire reached the upper floors.

I do not want to believe everything I read in the press. The papers,
particularly the online editions, publish a lot of false news. But
after learning what has been officially confirmed after the night of
clashes, I can't help clenching my fists: more than twenty-five dead,
including ten police officers. The others are protesters, several of

them women. The police say that their officers were hit in the head and the neck by sniper bullets: all of them were wearing bulletproof vests, so the unknown shooters aimed for the unprotected parts of their bodies. As for the protesters, some were killed by firearms, others simply beaten to death with truncheons by police.

And yet this bloodbath began with a peaceful march towards Parliament, intended to force the parliamentary majority to vote on the constitutional act that Volodymyr Rybak, the chairman of the Rada, had not even wanted to register. Then the jostling began, degenerating into fighting, and soon after that the first three protesters had been killed, and their bodies taken to the Officers' House.

The Berkut, mounting a counter-attack, took the barricades in Hrushevskoho Street, and seized Ukraine House and the October Palace. At the same time, its men began moving on Institutskaya Street, forcing the Maidanistas back. The retreating protesters gathered in the Maidan, about eight thousand of them. They set fire to anything they could find in order to create a barricade of flames. All night, there was fighting and gunshots. Who shot at the *berkutovtsy*? That is a mystery. Who shot at the Maidanistas, given that the Minister of Internal Affairs stated that the Berkut were not using real bullets? It would seem that, in parallel with the Berkut, there exists a group of plain-clothes officers, armed with sniper rifles, assault rifles and ordinary pistols. About one in the morning, they stopped a taxi driving Vyacheslav Yeremey, a journalist from *Vesti* ('News'), near my office at the corner of Vladimirskaya Street and Velyka Zhytomyrska Street: after beating him up, they shot him in the chest. He died in hospital.

The hospitals are overflowing right now. But many of the wounded are in hiding, from their friends as well as from strangers. They are afraid of going to hospital because the police have often abducted injured protesters from there to take them to the station, without offering them any medical care.

St Michael's Monastery and St Alexander's Catholic church continue to let people in so they can hide. Kievites take food and firewood to the Maidan. The Maidanistas are asking for glass bottles (to make Molotov cocktails), waterproof capes (to protect them from water cannons), and anything that will burn.

The protesters have now conquered – or, to be more precise, occupied – the central post office and the music school. The children are staying home; the schools are closed. The metro stopped working almost twenty-four hours ago. The official reason: the government fears terrorist activity there.

Many people were unable to go home this evening. Sasha, a somewhat hippyish friend of Gaby's, had to spend the night at our place. He and Gaby went to a hospital – I don't know which one – to help out. But they weren't allowed in.

The events of last night are reverberating in an awful echo in many other cities in Ukraine. Only Donbas – birthplace of President Yanukovych and his Party of Regions – has been spared, with no protests there. In fact, threats are supposed to have been made to anyone participating in pro-European demonstrations, with protesters promised a quick trip to Hell. But not far from there, on the Russian border – in Sumy, a city in the north of Ukraine – pro-European activists and other people tired of this regime are attacking police and the local branches of the SBU, Ukraine's security service. In Khmelnytskyi, SBU agents fired at protesters from the windows of their building. 'To cool down the hotheads,' their commander explained, failing to mention the fact that this burst of gunfire wounded three people: one woman and two youths.

Yanukovych is keeping his mouth shut but not budging an inch. Stupid bastard! Yesterday evening, the Maidanistas set fire to the Kiev offices of the Party of Regions; one person died in the flames. They also destroyed or burned two cars belonging to party activists. Then they trapped the Party of Regions deputy, Dmitriy

Svyatash, who has for the past two years been refusing to repay a $100 million loan from the Paribas bank. Terrified, he begged the Maidanistas not to kill him. They didn't. They sprayed him with tear gas and let him go.

Hatred is overflowing. It is born from a simple dislike of a Donetskian government that is both strange and foreign; a dislike that, by perhaps growing too fast, has become hatred, and is currently raging through western Ukraine, in Odessa, Cherkasy and other places. Meanwhile, Crimea is once again calling on Russia to take it back.

Putin is furious: Ukraine is undermining the Olympics. The world is more interested in Kiev than in Sochi. And today, the Ukrainian skiers refused to compete, in protest against the bloodshed.

In western Ukraine, President Yanukovych no longer exercises any power. There, even the police and the legal authorities have moved over to the protesters' side and are attempting to restore public order. In Kiev, nobody even tries to do that. It is quite simply impossible. And the SBU's announcement that it is going to carry out an anti-terrorist operation all over the country is hardly likely to reassure Kievites. Many of them – and they are not the only ones – think that the gunshots aimed at protesters and police were fired by secret service agents. The SBU's announcement itself contains some very worrying information: 1,500 weapons and almost 100,000 rounds of ammunition have disappeared in Ukraine. In other words, the SBU is warning us that we should expect more shooting. Who will shoot at whom? We don't know. But the ammunition is not about to run out, and anyone can be a victim.

Thursday 20 February

For the past two days, not only Kiev has been paralysed by the suspension of the metro, but the entire country. Motorways leading
to the capital are being closed; trains here are being cancelled; the
police are stopping and searching passengers. Checkpoints have
been set up on the way into the city, some by police, others by radical activists unconnected with the opposition parties.

In truth, the protests have little to do with the opposition
either. They began spontaneously, and the politicians jumped
on the bandwagon. The speeches of the three opposition leaders
on the stage at the Maidan did not spark much optimism among
protesters. But they do listen to them, if only because there are
no new leaders among the protesters themselves. The heads of
the nationalist party Pravy Sektor give newspaper and television
interviews, and want to stand apart from negotiations with the
government. That organisation did not even exist before the
protest movement started. In fact, it didn't begin taking part
in the protests until after the opposition parties, but now it is
everywhere, fighting: in Kiev, in Odessa, and on the Hungarian
border, in Zakarpattya. How many other radical organisations
are contributing to this violent aspect of the conflict? It is difficult
to say. But recently, the only way to distinguish a radical from a
peaceful protester is to see whether or not they have a Molotov
cocktail in their hand.

The protesters have already been through all the stages: from
the romantic phase, where everyone thought they could achieve

their aims within a few days, to a premonition of war, with revolutionaries covering their faces with balaclavas, wielding baseball bats and metal riot shields stolen from the police. Now we have entered a new phase, which can be summarised in five words: 'The bridges have been burned!' And many protesters on the barricades in Hrushevskoho Street have removed their masks, no longer fearing to show their faces.

The barricades have gone from Hrushevskoho Street. That road, blackened by the campfires that were lit all night long, has been reconquered by special forces. But President Yanukovych's great hopes have been disappointed. The special forces, rounded up from all over Ukraine, have once again failed to clear the protesters from the centre of Kiev. The fighting continues. Three dead men were taken back home to Crimea, from where several buses filled with police have come. Crimean politicians have reacted by asking Putin to retake the peninsula for Russia. Putin, for whom events in Ukraine have ruined the Sochi Olympics, preferred not to respond.

It has to be said that Yanukovych, not content with preventing Ukraine from sleeping soundly at night, has also disturbed the Russian president's sleep. During the night of 18 February, while the blood of protesters and police officers flowed through the streets, he phoned Putin and had a long discussion with him. Putin was asked whether this phone call really took place, and, if so, whether he had given Yanukovych any advice. He replied that he had not given and did not intend to give any advice to Yanukovych, nor the loan that had previously been agreed with Ukraine. It is clear that the Ukrainian president no longer has any reason for optimism. Nor has Ukraine, for that matter.

The opposition leaders are loudly demanding sanctions from Europe and America against the Ukrainian government. The government is treating all protesters as extremists and terrorists, and says that no government would negotiate with such people.

The only thing now that could stop the protest movement is the dissolution of Parliament and the announcement of a new presidential election, but it is highly unlikely that Yanukovych will take those steps. Now that the police and the legal system have proved powerless to stifle the demonstrations through repression and force, the president's hopes would seem to rest on the operation announced by the security services. In the next few days, we will see where this operation leads the country. One thing is sure: the secret services do not use rubber bullets or stun grenades. That is why we can only expect the conflict to escalate.

Russia wants war in Ukraine. Prime Minister Dmitry Medvedev said today that Russia would keep its promise to loan money only if the Ukrainian government is legitimate and effective, and only if Yanukovych stops allowing the protesters to 'walk all over him'.

Today, a lecturer from the Catholic University in Lviv was killed, along with several dozen other people. Snipers are shooting even at young nurses. One of these, Lesya, was wounded in the neck. Farmers are blocking the roads to buses of *titushky* and *veveshniki*. Some *veveshniki* are defecting to the rebels. A lieutenant colonel went to the Maidan and gave a speech to the people of Ukraine. Yuriy Pavlenko, the spiritual son of Viktor Yushcshenko, children's ombudsman under Yanukovych, has resigned. The head of local government in Kiev stated that he has quit the Party of Regions, and city mayors are taking down their portraits of Yanukovych.

There are rumours everywhere, each one more disturbing than the last, but the reality in this country is already horrifying: today, in St Michael's Square, two policemen were killed. Why? Who needs that? It is obviously the hand of Moscow, pushing us into a state of war. Meanwhile, European foreign ministers have been locked in a room with Yanukovych for the past three hours, trying to persuade him to agree to negotiations.

Friday 21 February

Nobody is celebrating victory. For the moment, there is no victory, and there probably won't be one. Ukraine has already lost. More than a hundred of its citizens have been killed, among them students and university lecturers, some of them women.

Yesterday, Liza told me that Theo had said: 'Mum, I think I should be in the Maidan. Can I go?' Liza replied: 'If you were three years older, I'd be surprised if you weren't there already. But you're fifteen, and we're all going to stay at home.'

New negotiations between Yanukovych and the opposition give hope, but only to inveterate optimists. Yes, Yanukovych signed papers regarding the conditions for a 'solution to the conflict', and more precisely for 'the cessation of hostilities'. The elections are set for December. So, in other words, until then, the man with more than a hundred deaths and more than five hundred wounded on his conscience will remain president, and he will fight the next election too.

For the participants in the protest movement, this agreement means nothing. Although the opposition leaders are trying to appear assured, they do not control the Maidan. No more than 30 per cent of protesters listen to their opinions. However, everyone is well aware that a peace agreement is necessary. Not a truce that will inevitably lead to yet more bloody conflict, but a real peace.

The country still exists, even if Yanukovych's supporters are working hard to divide it. The president of the Crimean Parliament has already been to Moscow, where he expressed the desire of the peninsula's inhabitants to become Russian citizens again. We won't have to wait long for the reaction of the Crimean Tatars. The Tatar people, deported under Stalin, and who only rejoined their historical homeland in the early 1990s after the declaration of Ukraine's independence, will use all means necessary to oppose Crimea's return to Russian rule.

In Kharkiv, the regional governor is assembling a congress of deputies from the south and east of Ukraine to study the possibility of separating from Kiev. The country is trembling all over – it is close to being torn apart – but Yanukovych doesn't see this. Right now, the problem he faces is remaining in power until the expected elections.

Saturday 22 February

Yesterday afternoon, Yanukovych signed an agreement with the opposition, setting the expected presidential election for December and a return to the 2004 constitution, which limits the powers of the president and makes the prime minister the essential figure in the government. The witnesses to the agreement – the German and Polish foreign ministers – signed the document, but Putin's representative refused to do so. Soon afterwards, in an interview, he described this agreement as 'a worthless scrap of paper'.

And in the evening, much later, Yanukovych fled. He seems to have flown to Kharkiv with his inner circle. But where could he have taken off from? It's a mystery. Boryspil is blocked by the Automaidan and the Maidanistas, and roads to the airport are closed. Maybe from Zhuliany?

In Kharkiv today, the congress of deputies from the eastern and southern regions is meeting, including those from Crimea and Sevastopol. They are going to separate from Ukraine – from Kiev, in other words. Yanukovych will probably speak and will be elected president of south-east Ukraine by this conclave.

History repeats itself. In 2004, after his defeat in the third round of presidential elections, a similar congress was held in Severo-Donetsk. After that, Yanukovych was summoned by the Public Prosecutor for several interrogations, fearing each time that he was going to be arrested. I don't understand why he has run away so suddenly this time. He didn't even stop off at Mezhigorye!

In the Kiev region, the dacha belonging to Putin's ally,

Viktor Medvedchuk, was burned down. People remember that when he was the court-appointed lawyer for the Ukrainian dissident Vasyl Stus, in the mid 1980s, under Soviet rule, he seemed instrumental in the imprisonment of his client. Medvedchuk has said he had no practical chance of helping Stus. Vasyl Stus died in prison.

A decree has appeared on the president's website, declaring 22 and 23 February as days of national mourning in tribute to the victims of protest acts. Because of this, all concerts and other public entertainments have been cancelled. In which case, how can we allow the opening of that circus named the Congress of Deputies from All Regions?

Monday 24 February

This morning, in the bathroom, I took a good look in the mirror. I feel like I've aged five years in the space of three months. I have to wash myself in cold water for longer these days, to return to a normal state. During the first two months, I would wake several times a night and listen to the silence; in the morning I would nervously approach the window of our third-floor apartment to look down into the courtyard where I always park my car. One car was burned in our street during this period, and several others damaged. All my neighbours ended up parking their vehicles elsewhere, so mine is now the only one parked at the foot of the building.

And then the apathy set in. I still look down into the courtyard each morning, but I am no longer fearful. I have lost the feeling that my car represents a certain value. The only essential value is human life. And it is in this currency – in human lives – that Ukraine has paid for trying to reconstruct itself once more, to cleanse itself of amorality and corruption. More than a hundred people have died, hundreds of others have been injured, dozens have disappeared. Among the latter can be counted, for the moment, the president and his entourage. But they are not dead; nobody has taken their most precious possessions – their lives. They are hiding, attempting to flee the country. A wanted notice has already been put out for them. For the first time in Ukraine, there are genuine criminals of the state! This is nothing to boast about, admittedly. Even in Bosnia last year, the president was arrested. Many people believe there is no such thing as an honest politician.

Meanwhile, students are occupying the Ministry of Education, and young artists and intellectuals have taken over the Ministry of Culture. Everyone wants the new candidates for ministerial posts to be elected with their agreement. The students have even made a suggestion for the position of Minister of Education. They are proposing that Parliament chooses between the rectors of two universities and the deputy Liliya Grinevich, who runs the Parliamentary Commission on Science and Education.

Parliament works tirelessly. A new government is being formed, and a new Cabinet. One of the leaders of the protest movement, Stepan Kubiv, was appointed president of the National Bank; and Valentyn Nalyvaichenko – a member of UDAR, Vitaliy Klichko's party, and a former comrade-in-arms of Viktor Yushchenko – has become head of Ukraine's security services. The judges of the constitutional court, who made the necessary decisions under orders from Yanukovych, have been invited to take retirement. The cleansing of the country has begun, but for the moment it is almost entirely in Kiev that the government is growing a new skin.

Yulia Tymoshenko was freed a few days ago. The event itself was greeted with euphoria among her loyal supporters. But when she spoke from the stage in Kiev's Maidan, sitting in her wheelchair, I and a number of my friends experienced a disappointment that, in all honesty, we had expected. Her long speech was made up of phrases and ideas belonging to the Orange Revolution. The country is moving forward, while Tymoshenko is stuck in the past, albeit quite a recent past. The almost three years she spent in prison have cut her off from reality. Many continue to put their trust in her. Many others do not believe in her sincerity, fear that she will regain power and start, once again, the game of tug of war. The return to the 2004 constitution, approved by Parliament, does not really suit her. But she says no more about it. It was when she was in hospital, under guard, that she gave orders to the opposition demanding that the powers of the presidency should remain in full, with all the authority that Yanukovych wielded.

They are not so dissimilar in some ways, Yanukovych and Tymoshenko. Of course, she is more intelligent, more elegant, more democratic. But their love of authoritarianism is the same.

Admittedly, Yulia Tymoshenko sometimes knows where to stop, while Yanukovych never does. The day after her speech, a rally gathered in front of the Parliament building, chanting the slogan: *Freedom for Yulia, not power!*

Perhaps due to uncertainty over Yulia Tymoshenko's chances of becoming the country's leading figure, Medvedev suddenly declared that Russia does not recognise the new government. Putin always seemed well disposed towards Tymoshenko; he even asked Yanukovych to liberate her during their one-to-one meetings. With her at the helm, future relations between Ukraine and Russia would be easy. On the other hand, if a representative of the forces of nationalism becomes head of the Ukrainian government, it will be difficult to have any kind of normal relationship. The Ukrainian ambassador in Russia has made no statement, while Russia pointedly recalled its ambassador from Ukraine to demonstrate its feelings about the Maidan's victory.

What will happen now? For the moment, Ukraine has other fish to fry, although everyone is concerned about a possible Russian military intervention in Crimea. Crimea is really the only pro-Russian region of Ukraine; the main Ukrainian patriots there are the Tatars, who number only 300,000. The Russian-speaking Slav population is about one and a half million people. The Party of Regions has infested almost all the regions. In Crimea, as in the rest of the country, all public offices – even those of district prosecutor and chief tax inspector – were assigned to people from Donbas, birthplace of the president and his party. Officially, the Party of Regions has around 1.4 million members, and 430,000 from Donbas alone, out of a population of seven million. But in general, it is a party of dead souls. Nikolay Gogol would have loved it. His character Chichikov would have had no trouble buying these virtual members of the party, subscribed by mines, factories, entire companies.

In the west, Ukrainians regret that the new government does not want to ban the Party of Regions or the Communist Party, as has been done in Lithuania and Estonia. The government says that would be undemocratic. At the same time, in the east, Russian-speaking Ukrainians demand the prohibition of Svoboda, whose leader Oleh Tyahnybok was one of the three opposition representatives to take part in negotiations with Yanukovych. Now that the country's Public Prosecutor is a member of the Svoboda Party, many inhabitants of eastern Ukraine can rightly be fearful. Particularly if they are state employees who surrendered, in the past, to the charms of corruption. There are thousands of such people: rich, corrupt, owners of large villas and fleets of luxury cars. But in western Ukraine, they aren't so afraid. They think that, being Ukrainian-speaking citizens, they will be treated more leniently by the nationalists.

And the danger does exist that the new government will seek out its enemies not on its own territory but within the Party of Regions. However, they should acknowledge, in all honesty, that Parliament is able to function and make decisions due to the fact that more than a hundred Party of Regions deputies continue to work there. Without that party, there would be no constitutional majority to legitimise the decisions currently being made by the Rada. The Party of Regions has renounced Yanukovych, as well as his inner circle, which it holds responsible for its problems.

Tuesday 25 February

Andrey Maystruk called me from the village. In Brusilov, a rally was held to demand the resignation of Shpakovich, the head of public administration in the district. Shpakovich appeared in front of the protesters holding his resignation letter. He immediately agreed to everything. He has been desperate to retire for a long time. He already felt that way when Yanukovych's people came and forced him to take over the running of the district again. In 2001, under Kuchma, he helped me set up the first regional literary festival in Ukraine; eight writers attended that festival, among them the Kapranov brothers, who have been active participants in the current revolution. We organised an exhibition of Ukrainian books at the Young Designers Centre and a presentation of writers in the Cultural Centre. The Kapranovs had posters printed, and the local authorities plastered them all over Brusilov, a village with a population of eight thousand. Nearly five hundred people came to the exhibition, and more than two hundred to the writers' presentation. We didn't have enough seats, so many had to stand. There were lots of young people. The next head of administration, put in place under Yushchenko, never wanted to do anything of the kind.

In Moscow, a Russian writer of Ukrainian origin – a science-fiction and fantasy author – declared that, in protest against 'Ukrainian fascism', he was banning all translation of his books into Ukrainian!

He must be seriously schizophrenic. I wrote this letter in response:

Mr Lukyanenko, I am told you are a fantasy author. It is strange that your imagination is not sufficiently powerful for you to understand that the Ukrainian people no longer wish to live under a system of total corruption, under an illiterate government that leaves behind it nothing but a pillaged and bankrupt country. Appreciating the degree of your concern regarding events in Ukraine, I would be happy, at a later date, to read the biographical work you will write on the fate of your literary colleague Viktor Yanukovych. If he manages to reach Russia, you must absolutely get to know him so he can provide you with a number of fascinating details concerning his life and his work. With two such fantastical imaginations as yours, you are bound to become friends! He could also give you another two or three names of poets and writers whose work ought to be banned from publication in Ukraine.

Wednesday 26 February

For now, the country is still far from being stable. Several times already, employees of the National Bank – currently controlled by the Maidan self-defence – have attempted to steal gold or huge sums of money in US dollars or Ukrainian currency. The last time, they tried to embezzle cheques worth several million dollars. If this happens in Kiev, it is not difficult to imagine what is happening in the provincial towns and regional centres. As strange as it seems, in Donetsk the situation is under the control of a governor appointed by Yanukovych, recognised by the new government. Then again, it knows perfectly well that these are likely to be his final days as governor.

Yes, in Donetsk there are rallies against nationalists and against the Maidan, but order is respected; the police in the streets defend the handful of Euromaidan supporters from aggressive local citizens who are convinced – who knows why – that, in the near future, their city will be occupied by the inhabitants of western Ukraine.

Paranoia is everywhere. Not only in Crimea and Donetsk.

In Kiev, the police are almost invisible. A few nights ago, I was driving through town and I felt as if I were on the set of an apocalyptic film. Not one police patrol car, not a single traffic police van. Instead, there were groups of men – fifty or so in each group, a mix of all ages – positioned every five hundred yards, all over the city, armed with long truncheons, scrutinising every vehicle that passed. They stopped some to check the identities of the driver and passengers. I was alone in my car, which is probably why I was not stopped even once, but they still watched me carefully as I drove past. These patrols continue to survey the streets at night. They are making sure that no one sets fire to any vehicles, that everything remains calm. During the last few nights, they have caught several thieves and handed them over to the police.

And yesterday in Kiev, I saw joint motorised patrols: one police car and one car driven by Automaidan volunteers. What struck (and delighted) me was that the Automaidan flag flew above both vehicles.

Thursday 27 February

This evening, I spent two or three hours walking around Khreshchatyk Street and the Maidan. I entered the city hall, I visited the tents, I chatted with people, drank tea, tasted the Maidan *kasha*, and met Kostya, the son of Dima Proshchakov, a business friend of mine who is in charge of buying paper for publishers. The traffic police are still attempting to confiscate Kostya's driving licence for 'refusal to obey an order to stop given by a law enforcement officer', and for having taken part in Automaidan activities during a few days when Kostya was, in fact, abroad – on a business trip to China!

This morning, we met at the Akhmetov Foundation to decide whether or not to extend the programme of grants for writers. The question is on the agenda for the second time. The first time was last year, following a declaration by a poet who had refused to 'take money from Akhmetov'. This time, we simply discussed the current situation and its influence. Holders of the grant – among them Marina Grimich, Katya Babkina and Oleh Shynkarenko – were also present. I don't know why, but my colleagues directed the conversation towards the lack of literary prizes in the country. They talked about promoting the grant award winners and their works, publishing critical anthologies and catalogues.

What nonsense! The country is in total chaos. In Crimea, armed men seized the Cabinet building and the Supreme Council. Yanukovych seems to have vanished, this time in Russia. The boxer Valuev, now a deputy for United Russia, Putin and Medvedev's party, went to Sevastopol. A delegation from Tatarstan is on its way to Simferopol (probably to negotiate with Refat Chubarov, vice-president of Crimea's Supreme Council, on behalf of Putin), while the Crimean Tatars are forming self-defence detachments to protect themselves from Russia.

The situation is very worrying. Olga Bogomolets and Petro Poroshenko have refused government positions. There is still no coalition, while things have to be decided today. I am deeply concerned. I already felt that way yesterday, but not to this extent. A video has appeared on the Internet of Berkut agents transporting the headless corpse of a protester. Furthermore, the Cossack Mikhail Havrylyuk – who was recently stripped naked by special forces in the middle of the street, in temperatures of -20°C – said that nearly fifty protesters were killed during events at the Mariyinsky Palace, and that two of them were decapitated. Our country has never known such horrors.

Saturday 1 March

First day of spring, but no one is thinking about that. We arrived in Lazarevka last night. On our way out of Kiev, the central traffic police station was empty: not one policeman, not one car, the windows dark. And only ten days ago, there were dozens of men toting machine guns, stopping every minibus and van to check their luggage.

The era of checkpoints is over. Yanukovych gave a press conference yesterday in Rostov-on-Don. And the whole of Russia, as well as the whole of Ukraine, listened to the presidential reject's incoherent speech, a speech in which this narrow-minded man showed everyone the true scope of his mediocrity by making insane declarations such as: 'Ukraine is our strategic partner.' I think they didn't let him go to Moscow because they didn't want to have to bother with a disinfection afterwards. Of course his presence in Russia stains Putin, but he doesn't care about that. What matters is that, having affirmed the legitimacy of 'President' Yanukovych, he can seize Crimea – which, in all but name, he already has.

Thankfully the Ukrainian authorities did not give any order for a military riposte. A silent but brutal occupation, with the whole world watching. Sergey Lavrov and the others say: 'What occupation? What aggression?' while Putin states that he has wanted to send the troops in for a long time. Well, now he has sent them, in violation of international law.

What will happen now? The Crimean Tatars do not recognise

Sergey Aksyonov's government of the autonomous republic of Crimea, as it was elected without a quorum, in an occupied Parliament, with unidentified men in uniforms pointing machine guns at them.

Today, the government district of Simferopol is encircled and the streets are filled with soldiers armed with assault rifles and machine guns. It is 10.20 a.m. and the television news has just announced that telephone communication has been re-established with Crimea. But all the military airports in Crimea are occupied.

Liza reacted without surprise to the appearance of satellite television in our country house. I explained that I had bought it because we may all have to leave the village if the situation becomes increasingly serious and dangerous. The calm and orderliness in Kiev are false. People everywhere suddenly have guns. Thieves and robbers are returning.

I went to the village post office, thinking of buying some *khrenovukha* – vodka with horseradish. I still find it strange that alcohol is sold in rural post offices; this never happens in Kiev. But this time they didn't have any. All the other products you usually find there were on the shelves: sunflower oil, tins of fish, buckwheat *kasha*, margarine...But I felt like buying a bottle of vodka and a stamp, so I could stick the stamp directly to the label and give it to someone as a souvenir...

What if Ukraine became civilised overnight and alcohol was no longer sold in country post offices? I don't believe that will happen! Something of the past must remain. Although, the less that remains, the better off we will be.

We went, without the children, to drink tea at Lyuda and Andrey Maystruk's house. They were watching the session of the Russian Federation Council on television. The council voted unanimously to send troops into Ukrainian territory! Liza was almost in tears. My morale is now as low as the Mariana Trench. I asked Lyuda and Andrey to change the channel or switch off the TV.

'We should pass a hat around Ukraine and collect enough money to liberate us from Putin!' Andrey suggested. Good idea. But he doesn't just need money. He wants everything. That is why he won't stop at Ukraine.

Sunday 2 March

Lazarevka. At six in the morning, the weather was misty and autumnal. I was thinking about the fact that, tomorrow, I have to send the results of the vote for the Russian Prize to Moscow. I am a member of the jury for the award, which has for eight years been given to writers who write in Russian but live outside of Russia. I will send the results, of course, but I doubt that I'll go there for the awards ceremony in April.

Russia, you can be proud! Your nationalist political tourists, otherwise known as Russian National Unity (RNE) – the biggest group of neo-Nazis in the world – hoisted the Russian flag over the regional administration building in Kharkiv. (The hero who achieved this feat is a Russian from Moscow.) At the same time, they beat up pro-Europeans, forcing them to their knees and smearing their faces with *zelenka*. The writer Serhiy Zhadan refused to kneel. They hit him on the head with a baseball bat. He is now in hospital.

In Kiev last night, three police officers were killed when they stopped an unmarked car. Nobody knows how many weapons are circulating in the country now.

The session of Parliament will open in about twenty minutes. I am now able to recognise the 'official' alarmist rumours that spread when there are military operations. Even reading the news feed on the Internet, you can sense which information is credible among all the thousands of propagandist lies.

Yesterday, at the Maystruks' house, Andrey phoned a friend in

Sevastopol. She told him that everything was calm in the city, but that on television they were showing horrors. Then I called my friend Enver Izmaylov, a Crimean Tatar and the best jazz guitarist in Ukraine. Turns out he's in Kiev. He wants us to go home this evening.

Two nights and one day in Lazarevka have given me back some strength and courage.

Monday 3 March

A scattering of snow on the roads. A light winter breeze, soon gone. At seven in the morning, I saw through the kitchen window the joint patrol of police and Automaidan. Four cars moved peacefully down Reitarskaya Street, heading towards Lviv Square.

On Sunday evening, we returned by car from our country house: my wife, our children and me. As we were approaching Kiev, I slowed down, as I always do, at the place where the traffic police have their checkpoint. I was curious to see the police officers who, in ordinary circumstances, are always there and sometimes stop vehicles. But, as on Friday night, when we were leaving the city, I saw nobody. The building was not even lit. There were only a few of the city's self-defence, dressed in green hunting jackets, keeping guard outside military tents that had been erected on the other side of the road, opposite the police checkpoint. No weapons, no signalling sticks. Even if none of my fellow citizens likes the police very much, due to their corruption, their absence provokes the feeling that the country is lawless. But a much greater worry is the occupation of part of the Crimean peninsula by Russian soldiers.

Tuesday 4 March

I slept badly last night. I awoke almost every hour and immediately switched on the computer to check the headlines. This morning, I finally managed to persuade myself: the war has not started. Not yet.

It's foggy outside. In the little courtyard across from us, a man wearing a simple jacket is crumbling a loaf of bread and looking around for pigeons. There are usually plenty here, but today, not a single pigeon.

My friend Igor has just sent me a text saying that Russia is withdrawing its troops. Then more news: Yanukovych will die from a heart attack in the cardiology centre at Rostov-on-Don. A rumour that is immediately refuted by the centre's chief doctor. The first piece of news floats in the air for a moment. We want to believe that there will be no war, but I am stupefied.

At 11 a.m., on Ukrinform,* the writer Iren Rozdobudko and I announced the start of an initiative entitled 'Call your relatives and friends in Russia and tell them the truth!' The number of Ukrainian journalists was insignificant, but there were two television crews, including one from China with whom I conducted an interview.

I went to see Petya Khazin. We listened to Putin's press conference. He lies easily, uses humour. The occupation was a joke. Military manoeuvres that had been planned for a long time. As for the threat to boycott the G8 summit in Sochi: 'If they don't want to come, they don't have to!'

---

* Ukrinform is the national news agency of Ukraine.

Wednesday 5 March

Someone said yesterday that, as yet, the only people to have profited from the revolution are florists and candlemakers. The Maidan and Institutskaya Street are piled high with bouquets of flowers left in memory of the victims. In every church, the number of candles being burned is a hundred times higher than normal. It's so that God can see clearly what is happening in Ukraine.

Can hatred act as a glue for the nation? Can it stop the country cracking up any further? I doubt it.

Second morning without war. But also without peace. The world is gathered around Ukraine, as around a sick child. They are trying to save it, to bring it back to life. But the number of cancerous cells in its system is now at a critical level. Not yet fatal, thank God.

Thursday 6 March

Still no war this morning. It is awful to think that those words may have no meaning tomorrow or the day after. But, today, all is calm in Kiev. Everyone attends to their own business. Motorists have become much more courteous with one another, but that courtesy is felt in a peculiar way. I'm the same: when I drive the children to school, I stop at the end of every field to let a car pass from some little side lane or to wait for someone executing an illegal U-turn. What does a minor traffic infringement matter when all the rules of ordinary life are being trampled underfoot?

The children are happier to go to school these days. They have plenty to discuss with their classmates. They pay more attention to the news and talk enthusiastically together about how the Ukrainian officer Yuliy Mamchur and his soldiers, all unarmed, entered Belbek airport, controlled by the Russian army, ignoring their warning shots. They also talk about how the captain of the warship *Ternopil*, when ordered by the admiral of the Russian Fleet to surrender, replied simply: 'A Russian does not surrender,' going on to explain to the admiral that he, Captain Emelyanenko, was of Russian origin, as was half his crew.

I too am Russian. Ethnically Russian, but living in Kiev since childhood. Different data suggests there are between and eight and fourteen million ethnic Russians living in Ukraine, and the word 'Russian' does not awaken any aggression in ethnic Ukrainians, nor does it make you look bad in their eyes. The first in my family to arrive on Ukrainian territory was my grandfather, in 1943. He died during the battle to liberate Kharkiv and his body lies in a common grave near Valky station, not far from that city. He died fighting the fascists, and now I hear the word 'fascist' directed at me because I have spoken – and continue to speak – against the generalised corruption organised by President-in-hiding Yanukovych, and so that the country in which I live can be governed by the rule of law.

Sunday 9 March

On 9 January, exactly two months ago, I returned with the children from Sevastopol after our winter holiday. We went to Foros, not far from Gorbachev's official dacha, where he was held hostage during the putsch. One year earlier, we spent our holiday in Simeiz, near Yalta.

We will not be going to Crimea on holiday next winter. And the outcome of this conflict will make no difference to that choice. I no longer want to go there. For me, Crimea has been sullied. Sullied by Russia.

The night passed without conflict in Crimea. Each morning, this headline appears on the newsfeed on the Internet. But I do not click on the link or read the text, because next to, above and below this headline are other headlines: the arrest by Crimean police of one of the leaders of the local pro-European movement; the abduction of the commander of the Ukrainian military unit against whom Russian troops attempted to mount an assault the previous day; warning shots fired at the observation group sent by the Organisation for Security and Cooperation in Europe (OSCE), who, once again, vainly attempted to enter Crimean territory; the destruction of coastguard stations; the entrenchment of Russian troops in Perekop and the mining of fields in the Kherson region; the firing of sub-machine guns at a Ukrainian reconnaissance aircraft by Russian Cossacks.

In Sevastopol, those same Cossacks beat up Ukrainian television journalists and a Russian reporter who was with them. Surrounded by all these reports, the phrase *The night passed without conflict in Crimea* sounds like a joke, of the kind published by Russian news agencies. Because, for the Russian troops occupying the peninsula, the night really did pass without conflict. No one attacked them; no one attempted to spray them with *zelenka*; no one threw Molotov cocktails at them; no one even hurled insults at them.

The liberators of 'Russian territory from time immemorial' feel fine; they feel at home. They act as if they have been told 'Hey lads, this land is yours! You can occupy it and stay here to live. You can build huts and houses wherever you like. You can keep machine guns under your bed. You can live here for a long time, happy and comfortable. You can grow and multiply, and whenever you feel too cramped, we'll help you decide who you're going to invade next for our common benefit!'

I have been watching various video reports on the latest events in Crimea, searching for one that I have not yet found: the traditional Russian TV favourite showing how the inhabitants of 'free' Crimea welcomed their Russian liberators with flowers, bread and salt. To begin with, it seemed to me the absence of such a report was due simply to negligence on behalf of the Kremlin's propaganda department. But, little by little, I came to the conclusion that it was still too early for Russia to show such scenes on television.

Because, according to the Kremlin's official version, there are in fact no Russian soldiers in Crimea. There are merely an unspecified number of sailors from the Black Sea Fleet, an unspecified number of unspecified Cossacks armed with machine guns, an unspecified amount of combat equipment, dozens or perhaps hundreds of Sevastopol *berkutovtsy* from the Russian side. But as for Russian soldiers entering Crimea as liberators against the Ukrainian menace, there are, officially, none. For now. Knowing how Russian television works, I am convinced that such scenes have already been shot and edited, ready to be broadcast when the moment comes, showing the world how these liberators entered Crimea while women holding babies hugged and kissed them, watched over by serious-looking old men who let a single tear of joy roll down their cheeks, young kids charging either side of the lines of Russian soldiers, attempting to march in time with those brave heroes. But all that is still to come.

In the meantime, we – citizens of Ukraine – try to understand how it is that this country, heir to the Soviet Union that vanquished fascism in Europe in 1945, could have taken the path to fascism itself, exploiting not only propagandist lies worthy of Goebbels but its own fascistic groups: very real hardliners from Russian National Unity (RNE) and other neo-Nazi organisations, which Russia is sending into the east and south of Ukraine to carry out pogroms, to intimidate and demoralise the population. The members of RNE, swastikas tattooed on their necks and arms, have no qualms about negotiating with Ukraine's regional governments and making ultimatums, demanding the liberation of their party comrades, arrested for having broken Ukrainian laws.

Anyone who has studied the history of Europe before the Second World War knows this scenario all too well. History repeats itself. Only this time Russia has not been able to – and will not be able to – find another Ribbentrop and another Molotov to conclude a new pact prepared by the Kremlin. This time round, Europe and Russia have switched places.

Europe is fighting against its neo-Nazi groupuscules, while Russia's are being fattened up and sent west, into Ukrainian territory. Simultaneously, patriotism in Russian society has been elevated to the point where it can easily turn to chauvinism. Twist it a little further and the next product of this approach will be simple fascism, and all those Russian schoolkids, brought up glorifying the cult of the great victory of 1945, will become utterly confused watching the brave Russian fascists protecting Crimea

– and possibly even, God forbid, other parts of Ukraine – from all that is Ukrainian.

I have a feeling the hundred Russian writers who signed a letter in support of President Putin will be prepared to postpone their literary projects in order to write new history books explaining to children that Russian fascism is good but that all other kinds of fascism are very bad. These writers should not be surprised, however, when they receive – from the government they are backing so completely and unreservedly – the insistent demand to produce novels and poems lauding the exploits of the members of Russian National Unity, and more generally of the Russian expeditionary army sent to occupy Ukrainian territory. Once these works are published – and they will be published, I have no doubt about that – then I am afraid that nobody will talk any more about the greatness of Russian culture.

Thursday 13 March

I am on an aeroplane, bound for the Leipzig book fair. Waiting for me at the airport will be my old friend Mikha, who will take me to the Nordic Hotel. This morning, I had time to drop the children at school. Afterwards, I went for a walk on Vladimirskaya Street: employees outside the bureau de change were putting up the latest currency exchange figures. The hryvna continues to fall, the dollar and the euro to rise. I passed a dozen or so adolescents marching in line, wearing camouflage clothing with badges. Among them, two young adults, the same height as the others. The permanent revolution continues.

But, overall, the situation in Kiev is normal, except for the Maidan and Khreshchatyk Street. Everybody goes to work, drinks coffee, talks politics and rails against Russia. During breakfast, before they went to school, Theo and Anton recited a nursery rhyme that is fashionable at the moment among children, listing the colours of the Russian flag: *Vodka's white, face is red, sky is blue, life's the best.*

Yesterday, at the request of my former teacher, I went to Obolon to make a speech to children in a secondary school. All the schools in the city have planned literary events recently in honour of the bicentenary of Taras Shevchenko's birth. But now, of course, it would be more accurate to reclassify these events as 'politico-literary'. I have already spoken at one such event, in School 91. That was simply a conversation about war, fear, the 'heavenly *sotnya*' – the hundred who died in February – and the future. A conversation with teenagers who asked questions that were not remotely childlike: 'What is going to happen now? How can we influence the future of Ukraine? Can the new Ukrainian government drag the country out of its current rut?' At the school in Obolon, the questions were slightly less political and slightly more focused on Taras Shevchenko. But I could see the same anxiety in the eyes of the children, as well as in the eyes of their teachers.

In the evening, we inaugurated the Turkish–Ukrainian cultural centre at 3 Saksagansky Street, opposite the National Film Centre. There were about fifty people, gathered in a small room. Children from the Meridian international school recited poems by Taras Shevchenko in Turkish, Korean and Azerbaijani. Enver Izmaylov played two songs on the guitar: one inspired by popular Ukrainian songs, the other by traditional Crimean Tatar music. Then we drank tea, ate eastern sweets, and had a long chat.

I left the centre with Mykola Kravchenko and Volodya from the publishers Nika-Tsentr. We decided to walk to the Khreshchatyk metro station. Across from the former Znannya bookshop, the pavements on Khreshchatyk Street have been ripped up and transformed into a series of walls and piles of bricks; the whole thing looks like a paintball field. It is time now to make the centre of Kiev look normal again, but the revolutionaries refuse to leave the city hall and go home.

Volodymyr Bondarenko, the temporary head of Kiev's local government, complains without rancour that he cannot, for the moment, restore order and free the city hall from the revolutionaries who are living there. There are too many different groups, incapable of getting along; some revolutionaries are demanding a free apartment, others a proof of residence, and yet others help in finding a steady job in Kiev. They took Kiev, didn't they? They got rid of Yanukovych. Now they want to be rewarded. But isn't a normal country, freed from corruption, the greatest prize any normal citizen could ask for?

The fact is, though, that revolution radicalises normal citizens, and – once radicalised – those citizens hardly seem accountable for their own actions. We need time. The country needs a period of calm, like all convalescents. But there is no calm, for the moment, because next door to us is Russia, with Putin, who is terrified by the Eurorevolution. He will do all he can to prove to the people of Russia that a government cannot be changed through revolution. And consequently, Ukraine is still facing a mountain of problems that will be very difficult to resolve.

Friday 14 March

Last night, thirty-eight self-styled 'warriors of Narnia', brandishing clubs and knives, seized a bank in Kiev, disarming the security guards and occupying the premises. They were not after money or documents. When the police arrived, long and somewhat confused negotiations began with the armed robbers. One of them said they had come to protect the bank from a possible attack; others claimed they were just passing by when the bank, for no obvious reason, caught their eye. When the talks were concluded, they returned the security guards' weapons to them and handed over their own to police, before vacating the premises. And the police let them go. They are now analysing all the recordings made by the bank's CCTV cameras in order to understand what really happened.

I don't think the warriors will be prosecuted. These young fantasy enthusiasts are the most exotic armed group of the Eurorevolution. They appeared in the Maidan in December, wielding wooden swords and shields, and at first brought a carnival atmosphere to the demonstrations. They distinguished themselves during confrontations with the Berkut. Later, their ranks were thinned out by snipers. Some were killed, others wounded. And the only thing that remains exotic about them is their name.

Now, like many other protesters' groups, and also like the self-defence detachments that formed after the revolution was victorious, they are looking for some way to use their social energy.

They 'pass by', ready to get involved in any situation that appears suspicious. Theoretically, it ought to be easy to find a use for such energy, in Kiev and elsewhere. The time for vengeance and for a new division of property has arrived. Many people mistreated by the previous government and its representatives want to recover – quickly, and by equally illegal means – what was taken from them.

The opposite situation also arises: people who were justifiably removed from their jobs under the previous government are claiming they have been victims of the regime, and are recruiting Maidanistas to help them get those jobs back by scaring away the people who replaced them. All this is happening quickly, noisily, and sometimes unfairly.

When will this socio-Brownian movement end? Difficult to say. For the Maidanistas, the revolution continues; it must not end. To leave is to betray the revolution. Nobody wants to be a traitor, so they are all seeking a pretext, a situation, an opportunity to restore justice. Not necessarily a historical justice, but a situational justice.

Saturday 15 March

We learned today that certain Ukrainian prisoners want to go off to war against Russia. I don't believe they really want to fight; they just imagine that if there is a war, they will be released and pardoned in return for their heroic zeal. That is what happened during the Second World War: battalions of prisoners were formed and sent to their deaths in the most dangerous and isolated parts of the front, so that they could pay with their blood for the sin they had committed against the nation. It is interesting to note that there are lots of recidivists among the volunteers, but no former police officers, judges or soldiers. Generally, the atmosphere in prisons and penal colonies has become somewhat overexcited. Many prisoners condemned for corruption have begun writing letters, asking to be held as political prisoners persecuted by the *ancien régime*. Not only do they write these letters to the prison wardens, but they are also attempting to prove to their fellow inmates that they are really 'politicals'. Perhaps some of them actually believe their own lies!

There will be a referendum in Crimea tomorrow. A Crimean man, interviewed on the television news, said he could not understand how a referendum could possibly be organised in only seven days. He compared its preparation with that of a wedding: 'It takes months to prepare a wedding, doesn't it? And a referendum is like a thousand weddings!'

In Sevastopol, people are rushing to withdraw their money from cash machines and spending it on vodka. Some are buying it to create a personal store. Others, more enterprising, have profit in mind. Vodka in Russia is twice as expensive as it is in Ukraine. It will be possible to make a profit by selling it for slightly less than the Russian prices when those prices come into effect in Crimea. Products with a long shelf life, such as semolina and tinned goods, are also being bought in larger quantities than usual.

Many people fear they will lose their savings in hryvnas deposited in banks; Russia will immediately put the rouble into circulation and the hryvna will be exchanged at a disadvantageous 'political' rate.

Monday 17 March

Half of Russia is joining Crimea in celebrating the results of the so-called referendum. On the Internet, Russian blogs testify to the vodka-fuelled enthusiasm for the peninsula's return to Russian possession.

The enthusiasm will last for a little while yet, but eventually the situation must be looked at more soberly. And in the cold light of day, who can be enthusiastic about a Crimea with a rationing card system for bread and other essential goods, as in Leningrad during the siege? Products reserved for inhabitants of Crimea and sold only upon presentation of ID proving the holder's place of residence.

Of course, the members of the various self-defence groups who have already received machine guns need not worry about having enough to eat. But those Crimeans who do not own weapons can expect some difficult days ahead. They are already frightened, and soon that fear will be joined by a new reality that no one will be able to describe as stable.

Tuesday 18 March

Putin recognised Crimea's independence yesterday, and that very evening the Russian television news programmes were showing a map of Ukraine with the peninsula amputated from it. The sanctions announced by Europe and the United States against twenty-one Crimean and Russian citizens provoked only bafflement and bitter laughter from those around me. But others say this is just the beginning of sanctions. We'll see. Meanwhile, events are progressing very quickly in Crimea, and very slowly in Europe. As if the news were arriving not by Internet but by messengers on horseback.

Weapons – and there are a lot of them – were being distributed all day long on the peninsula yesterday. The procedure is simple. One must simply be an inhabitant of the region – proved by showing ID with a place of residence – in order to obtain certification as a member of the self-defence; or, in other words, it's sufficient to go to one of the innumerable addresses provided by this organisation, and to swear one's love for Russia and one's hatred of Ukraine. After that, equipped with said brand-new certificate, just head for the local military commissariat to be given a Kalashnikov.

It is noticeable that the more Crimeans there are who receive weapons, the fewer working cash machines there are in Crimea. Many people are in complete disarray. The shops no longer accept credit cards. The banks are closed. The Crimean authorities are announcing the nationalisation of Ukrainian bank branches. The same authorities promise a quick conversion to the rouble and financial aid from Russia. But the Russian government has not said a single word more about the money promised to Crimea.

Self-defence detachments stop cars and buses all over the peninsula to check the papers of passengers and drivers. Anyone without papers is taken away and imprisoned. What are they looking for? Spies from Kiev, perhaps? The local self-defence consists not only of Crimean volunteers but also Russian activists and Cossacks. Soon the different detachments will be checking each other's papers.

The members of Kiev's self-defence and other revolutionary groups that took part in the overthrow of Yanukovych also have weapons in their hands. But those weapons were not distributed to them. That is why they have only one or two machine guns for ten people. And these detachments of revolutionaries roam Kiev, searching for some kind of outlet for their energy.

Last weekend, a Kiev businessman asked a Pravy Sektor patrol to protect the cellar of a building, where he hoped to install a shop. The building's residents, embroiled in a long battle with the businessman – who had no legal proof that he owned the cellar – called on a detachment of the self-defence to come to their rescue. While the two groups of revolutionaries were trying to clear up the situation, a car full of armed police also arrived at 23 Khalturin Street, but they parked further away and did not intervene in the dispute. A few of the revolutionaries fired warning shots into the air in an attempt to demonstrate the correctness of their opinion, but ultimately the affair ended peacefully. The businessman was forced to kneel down in front of the building's residents and swear that he would never again attempt to take anyone else's possessions. After that, the police asked everyone to end the argument, and the two revolutionary groups went their separate ways. Their weapons were not taken from them, and no one was taken to a police station. Peace was simply re-established. But when the first gunshots went off, the teachers in the nursery school in the building next door had immediately called the children's parents to tell them to come urgently and pick up their offspring. I had friends among those parents, and they were shaking with fear as they rushed over to collect their little Artyomka.

I am sleeping a little better now, in spite of all that is going on. Yesterday, the ophthalmologist prescribed eyedrops for me: after almost three months of abnormal sleeping patterns, my eyesight was beginning to worsen. Even once he had given me the piece of paper detailing the name of the eyedrops and vitamins I had to take, the ophthalmologist did not let me go, asking repeatedly: 'What's going to happen now? How are we going to live?'

That evening, I went to visit my Kiev publisher. We sat – him, his wife and me – at a small table and filled three glasses with vodka, which we drank with herring, fried fish and pickled cucumbers. Outside, the wind blew with a strength unusual in Kiev, hurling gusts of rain against the windows. We meet like this, my publisher and I, at least once a week. He and his wife prefer these soothing meetings to pharmaceutical tranquillisers. They always ask the same questions: 'What should we do now? How are we going to live?' His publishing house is not in operation any more, as the Ukrainian state owes him so much money. For a long time now, he has not had enough money to pay his employees or rent his offices. Every day, he says it is time to close the business for good. Yet, each morning, he goes to work in spite of all this.

As before, I go almost daily to the Maidan and Hrushevskoho Street, where barricades have been erected once more, covered with flowers in memory of the victims. It is now possible to drive down this street to reach the Parliament building and beyond, but the cleared passage remains narrow, just wide enough for a single vehicle. That is why traffic flows sometimes in one direction, sometimes in another. But, although this is one of the main central streets, in fact few cars go that way. Kiev's motorists have got used to bypassing the city centre.

People continue to come to the barricades, and Maidanistas

continue to live in tents alongside them. There is no way of telling which tents have been there since the beginning of the protests and which joined only after the victory over Yanukovych's regime. At night, there are lots of young people out on Hrushevskoho Street. They come here in couples, young men and women dressed in camouflage, some carrying clubs, some wearing helmets, a revolutionary badge pinned to their clothes. Detachments of young activists, which appeared on the square after that bloody Thursday, sometimes march down other streets. Something must be done with this mass revolutionary energy. So the government is proposing the organisation of a National Guard made up of volunteers to defend the country's borders. In this sense, Russia's aggression is a blessing, as strange and terrible as those words might seem.

Thousands of Maidanistas and members of the self-defence have already begun military training. When the radio announces this news, the sense that war is imminent is only intensified. Before, the news was merely bad, focusing on sad events. Now it is bellicose and full of enthusiasm.

In recent days, the governor of Donbas, Serhiy Taruta – a businessman and one of the country's less rich oligarchs – announced that he had paid for a twelve-foot-wide ditch to be dug along the Russian border and for a six-foot-high earth rampart to be built. Concrete fortifications have been constructed on this rampart, intended to stop the Russian tanks. The ditch extends over the entire border that the Donetsk region shares with Russia, a distance of at least seventy miles. If I ever describe this ditch in a novel, I will be sure to fill it with water and to populate it with crocodiles capable of biting through the Russian tanks' armour plating.

I had to block access to my Facebook page again yesterday, to stop Russians leaving me insulting private messages. They call me a bastard and a traitor. Weird that a citizen coming out in support of his own country's national integrity, and against an attack on it from a neighbouring state, can be considered a traitor in another country.

Wednesday 19 March

Today, Ukraine's naval headquarters in Sevastopol was taken. A military truck broke open the gates and women rushed in, screaming hysterically about the greatness of Russia, followed by Russian soldiers. The Ukrainian officers were disarmed, beaten and forced to their knees. One of them was ordered to burn the Ukrainian flag. He refused and was given a good hiding for his pains. The story about a member of a self-defence group being killed turned out to be untrue, but Russian television – which had broken the news about this 'murder' yesterday – did not retract it. The Ukrainian Ministry of Internal Affairs did, but only domestically. Two Ukrainian soldiers were killed. Ministers Vitaliy Yarema and Ihor Tenyukh took an aeroplane to Crimea, but Aksyonov stated that they would not be allowed to enter.

In Kiev yesterday, the Svoboda Party distinguished itself. Led by the deputy Ihor Myroshnychenko, a group of men stormed the office of the president of NTKU, Ukrainian national television, physically assaulting him and forcing him to write a resignation letter. Russian television channels immediately leapt on this as an example of the acts committed by Kiev's fascist government.

Dmytro Yarosh, the leader of Pravy Sektor, has filed a complaint with the Public Prosecutor against Vladimir Putin, accusing him of a common law crime. Now the Public Prosecutor must register Yarosh's complaint and issue a summons to the Russian president on charges of aggressive acts towards Ukraine, the murder of Ukrainian soldiers, and violation of the Ukrainian state's integrity.

The day before yesterday, Chubarov asked Parliament to recognise the Crimean Tatars' right to self-determination. It turns out that Ukraine has still not signed up for the UN's declaration on the rights of indigenous peoples. So not only must they now sign this declaration, but also recognise the Tatars' right to decide their own future.

I doubt anything will change now, but at least this provides some moral support for those among the Tatars who wish to remain Ukrainian citizens. They too suffered their first victim recently. On 14 March, Rechat Akhmetov, a 38-year-old father of three – including a little girl aged two and a half – was found murdered, his body showing signs of torture. He had taken an active part in rallies demanding that Crimea remain Ukrainian and had been seen for the last time near the military commissariat where he had enrolled as a volunteer in the Ukrainian army.

In the Russian press and in blogs, insults are again being slung at Tatars, who are told to clear off out of Russian Crimea. Almost everywhere, they are described as a treacherous people. All this while most Russians and Ukrainians who go on their summer holidays in Crimea and prefer to stay off the beaten track tend to rent rooms or apartments from Tatars, and to eat in cafes and restaurants run by them. We ourselves, each time we spend our holidays there – whether in Krasovitsky's dacha near Yevpatoriya or in Simeiz – always eat lunch and dinner at Tatar restaurants, as they are better in every way: cleaner and less expensive.

Last April, the writer Yurko Vynnychuk[13] and I stayed a week in Livadiya, in a Soviet-style retreat, to work on a novel together – a novel set in Turkey, Crimea, Kiev and Lviv. It was because of the presence of Crimea in this book that the authorities – in the person of Grigoriy Ioffe, deputy speaker of Crimea's Parliament – allowed us to stay there for free. When the parliamentary chauffeur, in a white Volga, took Yurko and me to the station in Simferopol, I asked him to find somewhere on the way that sold Tatar samsas, because I wanted Yurko to try some. Usually there are trailers parked along the roadsides, with traditional cylindrical stoves on top, and the Tatars stand close by to sell their hot, delicious pasties, stuffed with minced mutton.

Having not seen a single samsa vendor between Sevastopol and Simferopol, the chauffeur took us out on the Simferopol ring road. We bought five samsas and two bottles of ayran, and we immediately feasted on these delicacies, standing close to the trailer. Then we went off to the station, feeling happy.

Will Yurko and I write that novel one day? I don't know. But if we do write it, Crimea will be occupied by Russia, so the book's heroes can expect their adventures to be more dangerous.

For the moment, it is better not to think about those trips. From now on, those Crimean winter holidays will be consigned irretrievably to our family's past.

Thursday 20 March

This morning, the weather forecast on Ren-TV, as well as other Russian television channels, included Crimea, Donbas and Kharkiv in their meteorological map of Russia. I realise that a political map is generally used for these things, but surely it should be one recognised by other countries. Presumably this map is Putin's personal map, giving a clear vision of how he sees Russia's future. Or is the aim to prepare the Russian population for the coming occupations of Ukrainian territory? In that case, I will have to pay more attention to Russian weather forecasts in future, to check that Kiev, Warsaw, Riga and Vilnius are not included in their maps.

This morning also saw the liberation of Automaidan activists arrested in Crimea and the Ukrainian naval commander detained yesterday by Russian soldiers. The liberation of the navy's headquarters, occupied yesterday by the Russian army, was also announced, but that news seems strange. A liberated building in the occupied city of Sevastopol, itself part of occupied Crimea? And what now? Can the Ukrainian naval officers just go back to work, as if nothing had happened?

And – still this morning – Russian television and the Crimean press proudly announced the treason committed by the crews of three Ukrainian warships. They lowered the Ukrainian flag and raised the Russian naval flag in its place. One of the three is supposedly the *Donbas*, the command vessel of the Ukrainan navy – a sort of floating headquarters. If that is true, Putin must be cracking open the champagne at the moment: when a boat with such a name goes over to the occupying forces, that must give him hope that the entire Donbas region will, in its turn, fly the Russian flag from its local government buildings.

Meanwhile, in Crimea, police declared that everyone – irrespective of status or citizenship – must surrender their weapons before 30 March. After that date, anyone found in possession of a firearm will be arrested on charges of violation of Russian criminal law and handed over to the authorities. In Kiev, negotiations are still ongoing over the necessary disarmament of members of Pravy Sektor and self-defence groups, and for the moment police have not made any ultimatum or summons.

Friday 21 March

During an interview in Paris this morning, a French journalist asked me: 'What is Putin dreaming of at the moment? Does he have his own Ukrainian Dream?' Putin does not dream, I replied; he makes plans, checking each time for the reaction of the so-called international community, and pursues the execution of his plan in a dynamic way, step by step. Now that all the members of the Russian Federation have recognised the annexation of Crimea as fair and legitimate – and now that he has received the support on this issue of Syria, North Korea and a few other countries of that type – the essential problem for Putin remains the refusal of the civilised world to recognise Crimea as an integral part of Russia. For the moment, the peninsula has no legal status (as far as the civilised world is concerned), so there will be no investment there from countries other than Russia, Syria and North Korea. Its territory has vanished into the shadow of Moscow, but its new owner finds no particular joy in its possession. Usually, one is proud to show off a new diamond in public, but when that diamond has been stolen, it tends to be hidden away and looked at only in the confines of a dark room, alone.

Putin has to find a way to make Europe and the United States accept the annexation. There is only one way to resolve this problem: foment a civil war in Ukraine and encourage pro-Russian activists – armed, of course – to march on Kiev, accompanied by their Russian comrades. Once they are in the capital, this army should depose the Cabinet and the temporary president, as they are illegitimate, and replace them with representatives of the Ukrainian people, some of whom might well be the super-rich inner circle of ex-Prime Minister Azarov's government – a group that fled the country at the same time as Yanukovych – augmented by former leaders of the Party of Regions, which is currently not taking part in any parliamentary work but has not exiled itself in Russia, preferring to hide in its home region of Donetsk. The new government will announce the return – possibly only virtual – of the legitimate president, Yanukovych, who will sign (perhaps via Skype, from Moscow) a new treaty of friendship and cooperation with the Russian Federation. One of this treaty's clauses will state that the government of Ukraine feels only joy at the idea of Crimea's return to the bosom of Mother Russia. It will ask Russia to consider the peninsula as a gift from Ukraine in gratitude for the long and patient care Russia has lavished on its long-suffering neighbour and the constant economic and moral support it has offered, and also as a symbol of restoration of historical legitimacy.

What happens after that is, I think, easy to imagine. Angela Merkel, François Hollande and many other European leaders will emit huge sighs of relief and quickly re-establish their countries' economic and financial links with Putin's Russia. They will say: 'Oh well, it's over now. So, really, it was just a little domestic squabble, fuelled by too much booze. You know what they're like, those Slavs. But now they've made peace with each other, they agree about everything, and they're not going to worry any more about "little details" such as Crimea.' Naturally, Russia will leave some troops in the Kherson region, just in case. They will oversee the quality of the water supplied by mainland Ukraine to "Russian Crimea", to ensure that – God forbid – no crazy nationalists start pouring cyanide into it. To support these troops, morally and materially, other regions – Zaporizhia, Dnipropetrovsk, Donetsk and Luhansk – will also come under the Russian wing for a while.

That way, Moscow will feel more at ease, as it will prevent attacks on the train convoys transporting supplies to the Russian army in Crimea from uncontrollable nationalists and other criminal elements, for which the Russian government has yet to think of a suitably catchy and frightening name that it can use in the media. Finally, I said to the French journalist, you know how much work Mr Putin and the people of Russia have on their plates, with the former supporting the latter during every stage of the restoration of historical legitimacy, otherwise known as the reconstruction of the Soviet Union.

I believe such a plan existed, and still exists. But, judging by the current situation, Putin will have trouble executing it – or at least executing it quickly. In the Kherson region, as in the regions of Zaporizhia, Dnipropetrovsk, Donetsk and Luhansk, there are no Russian Black Sea Fleet bases. Nor is there one in Odessa, thank God. In other words, the Russians can no longer use the Black Sea Fleet manoeuvres excuse as a method of occupation. Furthermore, the Ukrainian army has been ordered to fire in response to provocations. Not that Putin ever intended engaging Russian troops, because their presence would immediately remove the word 'civil' from 'civil war', and that word remains extremely important for him. Putin's rampart in Ukraine is not only Oplot – the pro-Russian organisation in Kharkiv, whose name means 'rampart'– but a multitude of similar groups, militiarised and armed, organised or not, which the SBU, Ukraine's security services, bizarrely never seemed to notice during Yanukovych's presidency. Sometimes I have the impression that the SBU would not notice its own existence. But all that was before. Now, the situation has changed and the state's very survival is at stake.

That is why we must be ready for everything. We must not be surprised if, upon a key phrase broadcast by national radio (as happened in Spain in 1936, according to Soviet historians, with the words *Sobre toda España el cielo está despejado*[*]), a considerable number of Russian patriots advance from bushes in south-east Ukraine, Kalashnikovs in hand. It is precisely to prevent such a scenario that military units are rushing to the south and east of the country as I write. And during this time, all criticism of the government, no matter who makes it – whether it is the young deputy Oles Doniy or the super-eloquent and eternal objector Anatoliy Hrytsenko; whether it is aimed at the temporary president or anyone else – will provoke no surprise in me. Because, in politics, there is nothing simpler than simply talking, and nothing more complicated than simply acting.

---

[*] 'Over all of Spain, the sky is clear.'

Saturday 22 March

Ukraine had only one Crimea and only one submarine in operation, the *Zaporizhia*. The first was annexed two weeks ago, and the second was annexed yesterday. For now, we do not know the detailed facts, but the submarine was taken and the Russian naval ensign, the flag of St Andrew, was flown above it. Then again, that diesel-electric submarine, built in the USSR, is almost forty years old, so it's probably about time for it to take a leisurely retirement at the bottom of the sea. Along with the flag of St Andrew.

The weekend has arrived, and with it more Sunday rallies. In Donetsk's Lenin Square, nearly five hundred people, waving the Russian flag and the red banner of the Communist Party of the Soviet Union, called on Yanukovych to return and restore order. Pro-Yanukovych posters were stuck to the Lenin monument. I imagine Lenin, or rather his statue, feels comfortable and at ease in Donetsk. There, nobody is going to knock over his monument, even though he isn't from Donetsk himself. The police officers that protected this rally – from whom, I can't imagine – wore garish green body-warmers. I'm just thankful there aren't more aggressive mass rallies demanding unification with Russia. Either the pro-Russian activists are exhausted, or Moscow has stopped paying the travel expenses of Russian National Unity neo-Nazis who, last week, came once again from Russia to organise and support similar demonstrations.

A cat belonging to my journalist friend from Ternopil, Zoryana Bindas, returned home after three days away. It was all scratched and battered-looking. When Zoryana attempted to brush what remained of its fur, she discovered a bullet hole in its skin. The cat, it has to be said, behaved heroically. It did not cry or roll on the ground; it did not even miaow. Zoryana took it to the vet, who removed a projectile lodged almost half an inch deep in its flesh. When I heard the news, I immediately thought that this cat must have escaped to Crimea and been stopped by a member of the Crimean self-defence forces or by a Russian soldier. But it is more than six hundred miles from Ternopil to Crimea, which means the cat must have been shot somewhere in its home town. Thankfully the bullet was fired from a so-called 'traumatic' weapon, rather than a real one.

Meanwhile, in Lviv, a bag containing fifty-two new pistols was discovered next to a rubbish bin, obviously stolen from the police or the army. It is true that the government has ordered the return of firearms, but what it meant was that they should be returned to the police.

There was some good news for the police, though, as they discovered 42 kg of gold and several million dollars in cash during a search of the apartments and offices belong to the former Minister of Energy and Natural Resources, Eduard Stavytskyi. So at least Ukraine's gold reserves have been replenished a little bit.

This is my third day at the Salon du Livre in Paris. The Euromaidan girls, working as volunteers on Ukraine's stand, collected two hundred euros yesterday to help people wounded during the demonstrations in January and February. While the girls were working the stand, an elderly Russian emigrant couple poured out a flood of insults against Ukraine. Then a young Russian arrived, wishing to buy books and pay with her Russian bank's credit card. The payment terminal did not succeed in debiting the card, however. The young woman went away, then returned and asked to try her card again. But, for the second time, the machine refused her Visa card. At this point, a person standing next to her explained that US sanctions had now extended to several Russian banks, and that these banks' cards were no longer valid in Europe or the United States. The young woman was on the verge of tears. She left without another word. Thousands – perhaps even tens of thousands – of Russian tourists might now find themselves trapped in Europe without money, not to mention all the diplomats and company employees. Millions of citizens are going to pay for Putin's geopolitical tantrums. It is true that 70 per cent of the Russian population is in favour of the annexation of Crimea, but the Russians who travel around Europe are probably not Putin supporters. His support comes from people who have never been to Europe and who never use the Internet. People who only watch television.

Monday 24 March

There was a power cut in Crimea yesterday evening. The windows of houses went dark in Yalta, Dzhankoi, Alushta, and other towns and villages. The Crimean government immediately declared that it was an act of sabotage by Ukraine. Then politicians began accusing Ukraine of limiting the supply of electricity and promised that Russia would take retaliatory measures. Later, Krymenergo – the energy company responsible for the distribution of electricity in Crimea – apologised for a failure in its high-tension lines and promised that the failure would be repaired by morning.

Today, after a candlelit Sunday evening, the inhabitants of Crimea were comforted by some good news: from 24 March, the Russian rouble will begin circulation in the peninsula. Several containers of currency have already arrived, and soon a torrent of Russian money will flow into the pockets of Crimeans. The Ukrainian currency, the hryvna, has not yet been banned, however. In fact, it has been announced that the hryvna will remain in circulation until the beginning of 2016! In other words, Crimeans will need to brush up on their arithmetic, even if the prices of goods and services will now be displayed in both currencies. Nevertheless, from today, all state employees will be paid only in roubles, and company taxes will be collected in roubles too, which might cause quite a few unusual problems.

There is great confusion among businessmen in Crimea now. One is closing companies and shops because he used to receive all his supplies from Ukraine and send finished goods to the mainland. Another is asking the Russian government to exempt Crimean companies from tax. Representatives of the Russian government, tasked by President Putin with organising Russian territorial administration services in the peninsula, have explained that, if they wish to continue their activities, entrepreneurs must first of all register their companies in compliance with Russian law; once that formality is completed, they will be able to start work again.

The Crimean government is not letting up in its propaganda campaign. It has already raised the spirits of pro-Russian retired people by announcing that Russian pensions would be four times higher than Ukrainian pensions. The retired people believe this, and expect it to be true. Some of them think they are going to receive two pensions at once: a Russian pension and a Ukrainian pension. Yet for the moment, no one has received their Ukrainian pension for March. And in this instance, the Ukrainian government is not to blame. The Crimean authorities blocked bank accounts of the Ukrainian treasury into which Kiev has to put the budgeted money. So, for now, no more payments from the Ukrainian state are reaching Crimea.

If you watch Russian television, though, you would never guess the people of Crimea are concerned by this fact. On the contrary, the Russian TV channels continue to show citizens delirious with happiness at their return to Russian protection. Recently, an old Crimean woman interviewed on television declared excitedly: 'Now Russia is going to send us entire convoys of holidaymakers!' The term 'convoys', back in Stalin's time, referred to the livestock trains that used to take prisoners to the Gulag. The fact that this grandma thinks Putin is going to order Russian citizens to be piled up in train carriages and sent by force on their holidays reveals the mentality of many elderly Russian-speaking inhabitants of the peninsula.

In Crimea, in spite of the cult of tsarist Russia, the memory of the USSR remains strong, and the Communists are still influential. Most of the Communist Party's votes in legislative elections in Ukraine come from Crimea. Now that the peninsula's Communists are going to join the Russian Communist Party, the Ukrainian Communist Party is facing a bleak future. And what of the next tourist season in Crimea, given that the tourism industry is the peninsula's main source of income? That is an important question. For now, Russian travel agencies say the sale of plane tickets to Simferopol has fallen by 50 per cent since last year.

But the future for Crimea's grandmothers is not yet the future of Crimea itself. Representatives of the Russian government have given the peninsula's inhabitants one month to decide which country they want to be citizens of. Registration for Russian citizenship has been open for a long time. But for those who wish to remain citizens of Ukraine, the Crimean authorities are promising a multitude of problems. It has already been announced that it will be impossible to live simply in Crimea with a Ukrainian passport. Those who refuse to surrender to this logic will be forced either to leave or to carry out the formalities necessary to obtain a temporary visa in compliance with current Russian laws. Russian legislation permits dual nationality, but Ukrainian legislation does not. Many Russian-speaking citizens of Crimea want to obtain a Russian passport, but have no intention of renouncing Ukrainian nationality. And I am not only talking about those people who want to receive two different pensions at the same time. There are also people who have family in continental Ukraine or who wish to continue doing business with the mainland. They are aware that relations between the two countries are unlikely to be very friendly from now on. So they want to keep their Ukrainian passport to make it easier for them to travel in Ukraine, while their Russian passport will spare them a vast array of problems in occupied Crimea.

In Kiev, at the end of last week, Parliament adopted at first reading the law 'guaranteeing the rights and liberties of citizens in temporarily occupied Ukrainian territory', which governs relations between Ukraine and Crimea. According to this bill, a trip to Crimea not approved by the Ukrainian authorities could lead to three to five years in prison for a Ukrainian citizen, and collaboration with the Crimean authorities up to fifteen years. There is a whiff of Soviet-style Cold War in the air. I wonder who will provide official approval for travel in Crimea? The prime minister? The Ministry of Internal Affairs? Will I be able to obtain this approval online, the way I can get a temporary visa for Singapore, for example, or will I have to take all the required documents and queue for hours in some obscure office, then – as during the Soviet era – have to wait three months for the decision of a special committee? The surrealism that reigns now in Crimea is creating surrealism in Ukraine.

All the same, life in Kiev has more or less gone back to normal. As well as the weather forecasts, Kievites are also carefully following the news each morning on the exchange rates of the dollar and the euro. In spite of promises to open the European market to Ukrainian goods, the hryvna continues to fall. For now, the trend cannot yet be described as catastrophic, but it is certainly not encouraging. Rallies involving pro-Russian forces continue to be held in the south and east of Ukraine, but they are attracting far fewer people. Several major operations by Ukrainian security services – which ended with the arrests of Russian secret service agents in possession of weapons and money intended for separatists – have reassured the east's inhabitants about the SBU and the police's determination to genuinely defend the state in Russian-speaking regions. Members of Pravy Sektor and self-defence groups, who took part in the Euromaidan movement, continue to enrol in the National Guard, which is already assisting the border guards in their task in the east and north of the country. The flow of contraband over the Russian–Ukrainian border has suddenly fallen tenfold, and in certain areas has dried up altogether. Many people in border villages are extremely unhappy, as they have lived off this illegal activity for more than twenty years. But it appears that the border will no longer be transparent. An increasing number of politicians are talking of the need to introduce a system of visas with Russia. If Europe does indeed get rid of visas for Ukrainians over the next two years, then the visa system with Russia will become a reality. That will not please the inhabitants of eastern Ukraine, of course, who are used to going to Russia on a regular basis for work. But there can be no return to the old 'good neighbours' policy. That is clear. Personally, I am not frightened by the possible introduction of a visa system with Russia. What frightens me is a possible Russian intervention in the east and south of the country. It would be wonderful not to have to think about the possibility of a war, but a day has not passed without that possibility crossing my mind. Even the first stirrings of spring – the earth warmed by the sun, the flowers suddenly blooming – are not enough to distract me from politics. I would dearly love to turn away from it, though. And I am not the only one.

Wednesday 26 March

Lazarevka. It is pleasant to spend one night in Paris and the next in a Ukrainian village. No change on the eastern front, however. There, as here, the birds are undoubtedly singing more loudly in the mornings, thrilled by the spring weather. This spring has not awakened much joy in me, though, nor does it make me want to sing. On the other hand, the warmth of the morning sun does soothe me a little, keeping bad thoughts at a distance.

Liza left for Kiev yesterday morning, leaving Anton and Theo alone until the evening, when I arrived. She had told our neighbour, Tolya, about this, and he came over two or three times to check what they were up to. When I got here, at gone nine o'clock, all was calm and orderly in the house; looking around, the dirty dishes in the kitchen were the only thing that jumped out at me. Theo was busy painting some toy soldiers that he'd assembled himself, from a set we'd bought him for his birthday. He was using a special paint, very expensive; he spent 500 hryvnas – all the money he possessed – on it. But what matters is the result.

Before going to bed, we watched *Fierce Creatures*, a comedy set in a zoo: Michael Palin accidentally kills the American billionaire who had bought the zoo with the plan of selling it to some Japanese businessmen as a golf course. After that, helped by the son of the deceased, he makes the murder look like a suicide, which ends up as a sort of happy ending. Against the backdrop of the murder of Sasha Bely – one of the leaders of Pravy Sektor – by police near Rivne, the film takes on another meaning. Today, the police tried to prove that Sasha Bely killed himself with his own revolver, but those claims were instantly belied by a CCTV camera at the Three Carp restaurant where he was celebrating a birthday.

In Crimea, the Russian occupiers are having fun with blank passports that they found in the Passport Office. Already, fake Ukrainian citizens with brand-new passports have appeared, attempting to enter continental Ukraine so that they can support the separatists.

The day before yesterday, at the station in Strasbourg, I ran into Vladimir Maltsev, scientific director of the Karadag National Nature Reserve (in Feodosia, Crimea), who had gone to the Council of Europe to receive the nature reserve's European certificate. He got it, but now he wasn't sure where to take it. We had about five minutes together, just enough time for a chat. He was going home via Berlin and Kiev, while I was returning to Kiev via Paris. Maltsev told me he'd been contacted by Muscovite colleagues, with whom he'd studied at Moscow University. They were interested in rare plants that grow in Crimea, and they were collecting information so that they could include these rare plants in Russia's *Red Book*, the official list of endangered species. So Russia's *Red Book* is now open to Ukrainian grass and florets! I never would have guessed before that botanists could be used in politics, but now I understand: in Russia, everyone must bring something to the occupation. The army occupies the territory, while the Russian National Bank occupies the financial space, and Rostelecom the country's telecommunications. And the botanists...? Grass, plants, bushes and trees.

While waiting for news of Russia's zoologists and their assault on Crimea, I thought about our flora and fauna – and, more precisely, about details relating to culture and society. An interview with a disappointed winner of the Shevchenko Prize appeared surreptitiously on the newsfeed recently. The winner was complaining that Yanukovych's decree about the awarding of this prize to cultural figures had still not been signed by Ukraine's temporary president, Oleksandr Turchynov. Suddenly I remembered various documents that I happened to see during my Soviet and post-Soviet life, at the foot of which was typed the surname of some director, but with no signature beneath it other than an ugly slanted line, while above it was the signature of some other person altogether, the director's assistant or replacement. And I instantly imagined a similar document with Turchynov's signature above Yanukovych's typed name. Out of the question. That is too much like an Odessa joke.* It would be like asking Turchynov to pay back money that Yanukovych had borrowed. Anyway, going back to the Taras Shevchenko Prize: it has, during the twenty-two years of Ukrainian independence, occasionally shown signs of life – as when it rewarded Oles Ulyanenko, Yevgeniy Pashkovsky and a very small number of other figures from the arts world who were actually worthy of it – but more often emitted a persistent odour of sprats, an odour of the Soviet Union.

I myself worked for the Shevchenko committee in 2009 and experienced all the charms of this institution, from bribes offered in return for supporting such-and-such a candidate, to the perplexity I felt when the interim results of a secret ballot were publicly announced. In the last three years, the Shevchenko Prize has become the Yanukovych administration's prize. The winners were chosen in advance, from among the system's sycophants. The president of the Shevchenko committee spent more time in Yanukovych's office than he did in his own. Whenever a solid candidate was chosen who was considered unacceptable – like Vasil Shklyar, for example – the committee presented him as the prizewinner until the confirmation, but then he disappeared from the list signed by the president.

Through all of this, an idea has been growing within me: the

---

* The Ukrainian equivalent of an Irish joke.

idea that we should simply get rid of the prize in its current form and replace it with another prize, funded in a mixed way: partly by the state and partly (why not?) by a lottery, as is the case in Great Britain. The future president already has enough to deal with in terms of the country's economic and political problems, without asking him or her to sign piles of confirmatory decrees, prepared by the presidential administration.

As for the last Shevchenko Prize of the Yanukovych era and the capitulation of Crimea, I am sure that most of the prizewinners would agree that continuing the affair until its conclusion – i.e. until the awards ceremony and the payment of several hundred thousand hryvnas to the winners – wouldn't be ethical, moral or opportune, bearing in mind the country's economic situation.

Meanwhile, Sevastopol continues to surprise and delight. Not only is the city now run by a mayor whose election was not even carried out by a show of hands, simply by shouts of 'hooray!', but two days ago, on the beach of a town with the proud name of Crystal, a list of people banned from swimming in the sea was posted on a wall. These bathing sanctions are applied to Barack Obama, the president of the United States; Catherine Ashton, the High Representative of the Union for Foreign Affairs and Security Policy for the European Union; and practically every politician in Ukraine, including Sasha Bely, the Pravy Sektor leader killed yesterday in the Rivne region (who was listed under his real name, Muzychko). Admittedly, his name has already been framed in black. Which proves that Sevastopolites do actually follow the news in Ukraine.

Yesterday, Russian forces seized the last Ukrainian ship trapped in Lake Donuzlav. There are now no more war vessels flying Ukrainian flags in Crimea, a fact of which the Russian Black Sea Fleet's command is very proud. The same command announced that 80 per cent of Ukrainian sailors have sworn an oath to Russia, thus violating the oath they swore before to

Ukraine. One hesitates to describe those sailors as traitors, but I cannot think of another word. Of course I do understand that they were forced into a difficult choice: whether to swear an oath to Russia and serve in the Black Sea Fleet while continuing to live in Crimea, or to emigrate to continental Ukraine and continue to serve their country.

As for Russia, after dealing with Ukraine's navy, it is now attacking Ukrainian dolphins. Although, obviously, they are now Russian dolphins. Dolphins do not swear oaths. The national oceanarium in Sevastopol is already preparing to train its dolphins and sea lions in combat, in accordance with the Russian navy's new procedures. Russian military engineers long ago began producing and experimenting with special apparatus intended for use by dolphins and sea lions, with the aim of spotting enemy submarines, the wrecks of sunken ships, and even military divers wearing aqualungs. Back in the Soviet era, I've discovered, it was in Sevastopol that the zoologists and army engineers trained dolphins for military employment. Independent Ukraine had no money for instructing marine mammals in this way, but Russia intends to redress that situation now. And for Russia, it is all the more important as the world's only military training base for dolphins is currently located in San Diego, USA.

Thursday 27 March

The weather is wonderful once again. After breakfast with the boys, we worked out our schedule for the day, planning an expedition to Kostovtsy to buy grass seed for a plot of land that Theo prepared yesterday. This morning, I made Theo a sub lieutenant and Anton a sergeant. I remained a simple soldier, which is also the reality. A simple reserve soldier.

I would like to make time today to dig two patches for carrots and parsley, and to plant them before Sunday. The cost of living threatens to increase considerably. And what's more, our vegetables are organic. The morning news is as alarming as ever: Americans and Europeans observed a reinforcement of the Russian troops massed at the Ukrainian border, from the Chernihiv region to the Donetsk and Luhansk regions. Two military convoys equipped with war materiel arrived close to the former.

Yesterday, on the front line between the Kherson region and Crimea – in the no-man's-land separating the Ukrainian checkpoint and the Russian checkpoint – Russian soldiers handed over three Ukrainian officers who had refused to join the Russian army: Colonel Yuliy Mamchur (the hero of Belbek), Major Rostislav Lomtev and one other. Lomtev's wife and children were waiting for him. In spite of the rough treatment he'd received – the traces of which were visible on his face – he refused to go to hospital and left with his family in a private car. Mamchur told how, in the first days of their captivity, the Russians had attempted to incite him to commit treason, to fight under the Russian flag, but that in the days that followed they had merely stopped him sleeping by regularly banging their rifle butts against his cell door.

In Crimea, it has been announced that all citizens who are not officially residents of the peninsula must leave Crimean territory within a month – in other words, by 18 April. (Russia considers that Crimea became part of the Federation on 18 March.) Six thousand people have already obtained Russian passports, and special committees are currently examining another 20,000 requests.

Sixteen thousand pupils graduating from Crimean schools have registered to take independent assessment tests, the results of which enable higher learning institutes in Ukraine to select their students. Obviously it will be impossible for the pupils to take these tests in Crimea, so they will have to travel to continental Ukraine to do so. For now, no one knows where the tests will be organised, nor if the pupils will be able to go there freely.

The Ministry of Defence has distributed information about the emergency kit which all those called up for 'partial mobilisation' must prepare. They are recommended to take: a change of clothes, toiletry items (toothpaste, toothbrush, wet wipes, etc.), medicines for diarrhoea and fever, gauze strip, disinfectant, activated charcoal, a torch, a watch, replacement batteries, mobile phone. And – very important – a photograph of the wife and children, so the soldier will always remember who they are fighting for, if war is declared.

The Party of Regions is preparing for its congress on 29 March. Yanukovych and Azarov will be among the participants. The Russian politician and businessman Oleg Mitvol has revealed that his new housemate – the former Ukrainian president exiled in the Moscow region – left a few days ago for Rostov-on-Don, where he has already gone on two previous occasions to give press conferences on his legitimacy. I doubt whether our ex-president has gone for a third press conference, but it is possible that he will take part from there, via Skype, in his party's congress.

In Crimea, Sergey Shoygu, the Russian Minister of Defence, handed out medals 'for the reintegration of Crimea'. Among the first to be awarded was the self-proclaimed prime minister of Crimea, Sergey Aksyonov. Also decorated were senior officers of the Black Sea Fleet and members of the former Ukrainian Berkut suspected of having fired on protesters in Kiev. The new medal reproduces almost exactly the Soviet medal of 1944 for the 'liberation of Crimea from fascist German invaders'.

The Ukrainian Parliament adopted an agenda this morning, in the third round of voting, which includes a collection of unpopular laws aimed at saving the country from bankruptcy. If it is approved, the country will get out of this situation, but in the meantime life will be expensive and difficult. If the laws are rejected, the country may well collapse. In the evening, the laws were adopted in spite of votes against them by the Party of Regions and the Communists. At that moment, Parliament was besieged by Pravy Sektor activists, demanding that Arsen Avakov, the Minister of Foreign Affairs, resign in the wake of Sasha Bely's death. Pravy Sektor attacked the building, and the ground-floor windows were smashed. The Russian television channel Rossiya 24 was filming the event live, with each scene accompanied by an appropriate commentary. One of the young Pravy Sektor fighters attempted to steal a Mercedes parked near Parliament. He was wearing a balaclava; when asked why, he replied that Dmytro Yarosh himself had given him the order. But I doubt that's true. He wanted to steal this car because it had been 'paid for with his money'. Having failed to accomplish his self-assigned mission, he tore the Mercedes insignia off the bonnet, stuffed it in his pocket and ran away, leaving behind his comrades who were still busy seizing Parliament.

It is becoming increasingly difficult to distinguish Pravy Sektor's militants from ordinary crooks. Particularly as many crooks these days wear camouflage jackets and carry real assault rifles. Before committing a crime, they introduce themselves as members of the extremist movement.

After 6 p.m., I received an avalanche of telephone calls from journalists. Among them was a call from Moscow, the number withheld. 'This is the Home television channel. We're working on a programme about mixed marriages. Apparently, your wife is from Great Britain. If you're in Russia, we could record you in Moscow, but if you're in Kiev, we have correspondents there.' I replied that my wife and I have not talked about our private lives for more than ten years, whether to television reporters or newspaper journalists, Ukrainian or otherwise. The Home reporter then asked me if I could talk about my relationships with my friends and colleagues in Russia. I replied: 'I can't say your proposal particularly interests me.' He tried again to come up with a new phrasing that might appeal to me, but I bade him farewell and hung up.

Meanwhile, Russia has declared that its troops massed at the Ukrainian border are not preparing for an attack, but simply taking part in very large-scale military exercises, taking in not only the western part of Russia, but also the Sea of Japan coastline. Aeroplanes will practise bombing targeted enemy objectives, firing missiles at those same objectives, and many other things. After this, I expect, the real manoeuvres will begin, the same ones that took place in Crimea and which, according to Putin, ended on 7 March. And we all know how they ended. The UN's General Assembly decided today to treat the result of those manoeuvres as illegitimate.

Tymoshenko, who has decided to stand in the presidential elections (did anyone ever doubt it?), has begun her publicity campaign with the online publication of a telephone conversation she had with the deputy Nestor Shufrych. Having spent two years in hospital watched by CCTV cameras, one expects her to have learned perfect self-control. Which is why all the immoderate language she uses to attack Putin and Russia during this friendly conversation with a deputy from Yanukovych's party suggests that she said all of this with the express intention of publishing her words on the Internet. Who recorded the phone call? The Russian FSB (the Federal Security Service of the Russian Federation) or Yulia herself? Not that it matters. It is simply the start of the presidential election campaign, during which she must come across as tougher and more radical than Yarosh and his Pravy Sektor.

Friday 28 March

The sun has been shining since early this morning. There is a slight wind. The boys are already watering the lawn they sowed yesterday. Liza and Gaby are on their way to us. Today, we will all be together, even if Gaby would rather not be: she always prefers staying in Kiev, without her parents. The morning has been strangely calm. It is already gone eleven, and the cockerels are still crowing.

In Crimea, the pro-Russian self-defence movement seized a wine-making plant in Livadia yesterday. I hope they took something to eat! Meanwhile, Russian officials in charge of the sale of alcoholic drinks are already selling licences for producers of spirits and wines, so that the manufacture and sale of alcohol can comply with Russian regulations and the drinks can be exported to Russia. More than forty licences were sold yesterday, but – according to a representative of Rosalkogol, the federal department governing the alcohol market – there was a much higher number of applicants.

Sergey Aksyonov is in thrall to a new obsession: creating his own Las Vegas, with dozens of casinos and luxury hotel-restaurants. Presumably this is a long-standing dream, as gambling and casinos are banned in Ukraine, even if, of course, there used to be lots of secret casinos, and there are probably quite a few still in existence.

Also yesterday, in Crimea, registration of requests for Russian passports was suspended. No explanation was offered, except that it will be a while before the process of transforming Crimea's inhabitants into Russian citizens begins again. Perhaps there weren't enough blank passports, or perhaps officials were simply terrified by the volume of work and are waiting for a detachment of Muscovite civil servants with experience in passports to be parachuted into Crimea. However, it is possible that this pause is connected to Putin's fears. Yesterday, during a meeting with the Federation Council, the Russian president said that all citizens with non-Russian nationality must declare that fact. In the event that their nationality is not communicated, the offender will be given either an administrative or a criminal punishment. In Ukraine, where dual nationality is prohibited, there is no punishment for holding a second passport. And now various Ukrainian politicians are advising the inhabitants of Crimea who do not wish to give up Ukrainian nationality to tell police they have lost their Ukrainian passport. The idea being that they won't have to hand it over to Russian authorities when they receive the passport that makes them a Russian citizen.

The Russian Education Minister has prepared a short teaching manual for Russian schools, and it contains a special lesson devoted to 'the reintegration of Crimea in the Russian Federation'. This manual offers a brief history of Crimea, but says nothing about the Crimean Tatars and their deportation by Stalin. So, once again, the Tatars do not exist as far as Russia is concerned. And not a word about them in the Russian TV reports. Is the Kremlin preparing some new decree declaring their return from deportation illegal?

Russian military manoeuvres are continuing on Ukraine's borders. In the evening, freight trains brought brand-new Russian T-90 tanks. In a separate delivery, ten 3S-82 mobile propaganda stations arrived at the border. These armoured vehicles with giant megaphones have hardly been used at all since the Second World War. And during that conflict, this type of machine was mostly used by the German army to call upon Soviet soldiers and resistance fighters to surrender. These stations can broadcast messages over almost four miles. They can either play tape-recorded messages or someone can read a text into a microphone with a wire over five hundred yards in length. In other words, the propagandist does not have to be inside the vehicle as they broadcast their message; they could be hiding far away in some bushes, their voice amplified at 1000W, so that if, by chance, a shell were to hit the station, they would remain alive and would not become voiceless. I wonder where the Russian command will find the speakers they need to operate these military propaganda tools. Maybe from Russian television? There is no lack of faithful, pro-Putin patriots, such as presenter Sergey Dorenko, who – during a talk show on the Russian–Ukrainian conflict yesterday – called upon the government to put the Ukrainian leaders and politicians against the wall and open fire on them with machine guns.

Saturday 29 March

Lazarevka. Sunshine and cold wind since this morning. The wind is blowing from the north. I want to believe it won't bring any Russian parachutists. Gaby insisted I drive her to Brusilov, so that she can take the bus back to Kiev and enjoy life there without us. I bought fresh bread and vegetables. For some physical exercise, I dug up earth to plant onions and finished chopping wood.

Russia has decided to return the *Zaporizhia*, Ukraine's only submarine. As the commander of the Black Sea Fleet explained, the *Zaporizhia* is in poor condition; it is forty years old, and it has not gone to sea for over twenty years. Its crew were offered the chance to serve in the Russian Federation navy. Instead of a submarine that doesn't work, they were promised six submarines that do work, powered by diesel and electricity, which are currently being built in a naval shipyard in St Petersburg. The Black Sea will soon be swarming with Russian submarines. The poor dolphins will feel cramped.

Putin has furthermore decided to return to Ukraine all old or damaged equipment seized from military bases in Crimea. This is strange, as scrap metal is expensive and he could easily resell it in China. The only problem would be delivering all this stuff to the Chinese scrap-metal merchants.

The day's political event is Vitaliy Klichko's declaration, at his party's congress, that he will support Petro Poroshenko as a candidate for the Ukrainian presidency. This is a good, noble gesture. As for Klichko, he intends to stand in Kiev's mayoral election.

A rally for the Batkivshchyna Party was held in St Sophia Square, during which, as expected, after speeches by the former Georgian president, Mikheil Saakashvili, and a few others, Yulia Tymoshenko appeared onstage, limping slightly in very high heels, and declared publically – of course – that she is going to stand in the presidential elections. The old ladies who adore her wept affectionately as they listened to her passionate if somewhat outdated revolutionary speech.

In Kharkiv, the Party of Regions congress began, with journalists not admitted. So, to begin with, the news filtered through by word of mouth from the activists leaving the meeting, particularly from those unhappy with the decisions that had been taken. Only one candidate was nominated to run for president: the former governor of the Kharkiv region, Mykhailo Dobkin. I think they chose him deliberately so he would lose the election. The other candidates are more popular, simply by dint of being more intelligent and charismatic than Dobkin. Serhiy Tihipko, who had hoped to be chosen as the Party of Regions' sole candidate – and had been one of the first to hand over the necessary documents to the TsIK, the central electoral committee, so that he could take part in the elections – declared onstage at the congress that he would not withdraw his candidacy. Two other members had provided the TsIK with the required papers, without having consulted their party. One of them was the principal Kremlin agent Oleg Tsarov, who didn't even attend the congress. He may nevertheless qualify on the grounds of history: he expelled from the party ex-President Yanukovych, ex-Prime Minister Azarov, ex-Deputy Prime Minister (and Yanukovych's personal banker) Serhiy Arbuzov, and former Minister of Revenue and Duties Aleksandr Klimenko. The former president's whole mafia family, in other words. But if Party of Regions' members think they have cleansed the party by doing this, they are seriously deluded.

Altogether, a total of seventeen people have already declared their intention to become president of Ukraine. One of them is Pravy Sektor leader Dmytro Yarosh, who is driven around in a car taken from Yanukovych's collection. That is just too revolutionary. Thankfully the revolutionaries who seized Yanukovych's wardrobe in February were not representatives of Pravy Sektor. I wish I had seen those people leaving the former president's former residence wearing his oversized jackets. Yanukovych was indeed a president of great substance, in the truest meaning of the term. His suits were probably made to measure. We should find his tailor, and have a chat with him. What must it be like to measure a president just with a tape measure?

Only in Italy are elections as carnivalesque as they are here. Except, in Ukraine, the carnival is always anarchistic, and more or less uncontrollable.

The Maystruks came to dinner this evening. We drank a home-made blackberry wine given to us by Andrey and Lyuda, and ate a curry, followed by some cheese I had brought back from France last week. When we went out to accompany them to the gate, we stopped for a moment to admire the very dark sky, scattered with startlingly bright stars. It was an amazing sight, even if the air had grown cold with nightfall and a harsh wind was once again blowing from the north.

Monday 31 March

I have just arrived in London. Yesterday, in the countryside, Liza planted onions, but there is still a lot of gardening to be done. Our stay in Lazarevka – one week for the boys and four days for Liza and me – was a bucolic festival of work and relaxation. I would have loved to stay there longer: it is the perfect time of year, with nature awakening, the birds giving a concert every morning, echoed by the cockerels who are still celebrating the sunrise at ten in the morning. But at four o'clock yesterday afternoon, we went home to Kiev.

In the evening, we walked to Podil to see Eric, a very hospitable French diplomat who made us cocktails of his own invention – champagne with pomegranate juice, Koktebel cognac and coriander seeds – which he has christened Free Crimea. Of course, this cocktail really needed Crimean champagne, but in the absence of anything better, we had to make do with French wine. The actor and director Sergey Masloboyshchikov and the documentary-maker Sveta Zinovyeva were there. We spent three hours talking about the Maidan: all the incidents and events, etc. It was gone midnight when we took a taxi home.

At 7 a.m. I took another taxi, this time to the airport. On the way there, the cabbie and I strongly criticised Tymoshenko and praised Poroshenko. We also talked about justice. He remembered making several journeys on the night of the shootings – 18 February – ferrying around an obviously delinquent young man, not from Kiev, to the most expensive restaurants and clubs in the city.

Masloboyshchikov described how he had been at the corner of Vladimirskaya Street and Velyka Zhytomyrska Street, in front of the belfry, when Yeremey, the journalist from *Vesti*, was killed. The actor saw several hundred baseball-bat-wielding *titushky* pass close by. He wasn't wearing any Ukrainian badges or Maidan insignia, so he wasn't worried. In Rylsky Street, four young members of the self-defence movement came out to meet him. They had just been fighting with the *titushky*, and they asked him in Ukrainian where those thugs had gone. He told them there were hundreds of *titushky* in that direction. So the young men decided to change their plans and to return to Streletskaya Street. Three minutes later, another ten self-defence members came towards him. Masloboyshchikov explained the situation to them too. They asked about the four he had just seen, so he sent the new group to join them in Streletskaya Street. Later, he learned that Yeremey had attempted to photograph the *titushky* from his taxi: that was why they dragged him from the vehicle, beat him up and shot him in the chest.

Tuesday 1 April

New revolutionary scandals in Kiev. Journalists followed Avakov's cortège in their own cars, filming him speeding through the city's streets at over 110 mph while one of his escort vehicles pushed cars blocking his passage off the road. Yesterday, one of Pravy Sektor's 'soldiers', fairly drunk, started shooting in the Maidan after a disagreement with an activist from the self-defence movement. The city froze in horror at the sound of the sudden burst of Kalashnikov fire. Result: three wounded, including the assistant to the city's interim mayor. A young man from the self-defence group was hit in both lungs. After firing, the Pravy Sektor gunman took refuge in the Dnipro Hotel in European Square, just over three hundred yards from the Maidan, where that paramilitary organisation has set up its headquarters. The police surrounded the hotel and began talks with Pravy Sektor aimed at making the activists give up their weapons and hand over the culprit. The gunman was finally arrested. After several hours of negotiations, about two hundred members of the party were allowed to leave the hotel, taking their belongings with them – among them long objects wrapped in thick cloth which they loaded into trucks before leaving, escorted by the police. The police were quick to claim that Pravy Sektor left their weapons in the hotel, but that is hard to believe. According to the official news, the group was taken to a youth holiday camp in the Kiev region. On Hrushevskoho Street, not far from the Dnipro Hotel, the authorities attempted to reach an agreement with the self-defence movement for the dismantling of the barricades. But the barricades are being guarded by the representatives of various *sotnyas* incapable of agreeing on anything. To begin with, they promised to remove the barricades to allow traffic to pass forty days after the deaths of combatants from the 'heavenly *sotnya*'. But now, they have changed their minds. Two tractors and a dump truck arrived, sent by the city government to restore order. Result: one of the tractor drivers was ejected from his vehicle, and self-defence activists descended on it like flies on a pot of honey, taking it for a spin on Khreshchatyk Street. The anarchy that reigns here is beginning to grate. But I predicted all of this a month ago. It is very difficult to return revolutionaries to a normal life. How can we do this peacefully? Right now, it is hard to see a way.

The government's attitude towards the Maidanistas is becoming harsher. 'The law-abiding Maidanistas have joined the National Guard or reinforced the self-defence groups on the Russian border, in the north and the east of the country,' Avakov declared. 'Those who remain in Kiev are the ones who do not want to defend the nation and those who are afraid to go to our borders because the danger there is real.'

Parliament today took the decision to immediately disarm all illegal organisations. The measure is aimed at ordinary criminals, revolutionaries, and revolutionary criminals like Sasha Bely.

In Crimea, there are reports about the presence of Judge Rodion Kireyev, who had fled Kiev. He was the one who took the decision to incarcerate Yulia Tymoshenko.

In Donetsk, the governor Serhiy Taruta gave owners of illegal mines one month to comply with regulations. There are more than 160 secret pits in the region, with miners working in dangerous conditions. Last year, more than 150 people died in such pits. The miners accept this dangerous work because they are paid in cash, every day, on the basis of how much coal they extract. Employment rules are not respected, of course, and often the owners of these mines do not even know the names of their employees, so when a tunnel collapses on the miners, their families are the only ones who care about trying to find them. The bosses disappear straight away.

The presidential campaign is gathering speed. The candidate for Yanukovych's former party, Mykhailo Dobkin, has published his manifesto. This former separatist is now describing Ukrainian neo-separatists as 'marginals'. If things go on like this, the regionalists and communists will soon be vying for the title of Ukraine's greatest patriot.

Many public figures are calling on Tymoshenko to withdraw her candidacy for the presidential elections, but she has not reacted. In all probability, she will fight to the end, causing more division in the democrats' ranks. Particularly if she starts criticising or vilifying Petro Poroshenko during the electoral campaign. And she is capable of that.

The Russian prime minister, Medvedev, arrived in Crimea and began by promising to send thirty-three aeroplanes full of holidaymakers from Russia each day. Why thirty-three exactly? Is there some connection with orthodoxy? One plane for every year spent on earth by Jesus Christ, perhaps? Aeroflot has already announced that it is lowering its fares to Crimea, as well as increasing the number of flights. Now they just have to find people to fill the planes with! And, probably to make up for the shortfall in profits caused by the lowered flight prices, Russia announced an increase in the price of gas for Ukraine. From today, the price has gone up by 43 per cent. Why has the word 'gas' become synonymous with Russia over the last ten years? Even back in the time of the Orange Revolution, there were jokes on the subject: 'Moscow is the capital of Gazprom', for instance, or 'Russia was the name of the country on which another state has been constructed: Gazprom'. The meaning of the old proverb *Here breathes the Russian spirit, here is the sweet smell of Russia* has changed forever.

Wednesday 2 April

Yesterday, Tymoshenko said she had no intention of withdrawing her candidacy and that she was already supporting Poroshenko enough by constantly buying his sweets. (Poroshenko runs the largest confectionery company in Ukraine.) After that, I had an awful dream: on President Tymoshenko's orders, the members of Pravy Sektor were being arrested in the middle of the night, and those who managed to escape took refuge in the forest. Tymoshenko had full powers, in spite of a return to the 2004 constitution, and her prime minister – completely under her control – turned obediently whenever she yelled 'Hey!' at him.

This morning, another deputy quit Yulia Tymoshenko's party; one of its most active members this time, Mykola Tomenko. Although he has asked people not to imagine that his resignation has anything to do with Tymoshenko's decision to stand for the presidential elections, it is difficult to do otherwise. In Odessa, the 'capital of humour', the annual Humorina Festival took place yesterday, with the slogan *Everyone laughs in the same language!*

Also yesterday, Russia cancelled negotiations with Ukraine set for 4 April in Minsk, the capital of Belarus. The war continues, and will go on until the presidential elections take place on 25 May, or until Russia definitively succeeds in sabotaging them.

Medvedev has talked about creating a Ministry of Crimean Affairs in Moscow. In Crimea, officials promise to replace Ukrainian registration plates with Russian ones any day now. I wonder how motorists will be punished if they continue to drive a car with the old plates.

The Ministry of Internal Affairs announced that a first suspect was arrested on 21 March for the murder of Yeremey, the *Vesti* journalist. But neither his name nor any other details have been made public.

Thursday 3 April

I went to the Bacchus restaurant this evening. The owner, Sasha Savchenko, was sitting with a young female fashion photographer from Kharkiv. We talked about Pravy Sektor. Savchenko's interest in that party has diminished since the links between Dmytro Yarosh and the leadership of the SBU – as well as Yarosh's old friendship with Valentyn Nalyvaichenko, head of the SBU from 2005 to 2010 – were made public. At the same time, reports circulated that Pravy Sektor maintained relations with the Russian FSB, but those accusations were based purely on the fact that Russia used the activities of the movement's militants, such as the recently killed Sasha Bely, to feed its propaganda campaign against Ukraine.

The boy wounded two days ago in the Maidan by a Pravy Sektor activist has died in hospital. If the revolutionaries had just gone home after the revolution, none of this would have happened. I fear that the passivity of the police – who either don't want to or are afraid to become more actively involved in disarming the revolutionaries – will lead to further casualties. The Maidanistas, who still live in tents in the square, are looking for action, particularly those with guns. Some of them believe that the only way to quickly improve the situation in Ukraine is through the use of assault rifles.

Friday 4 April

At 11 a.m., I went to the Soros Foundation, for a meeting of the supervisory board of the Humanitarian Justice initiative. We examined documents and requests relating to victims from the Maidan period. We also discussed the unpleasant situations created by certain individuals who are attempting to obtain money, supposedly for their care, from several organisations at the same time. It's a shame that all these victims' aid funds refuse to create a single database relating to the injured in such a way that everyone would know who had already received money for their treatment and who still needed it. More than 170 victims are currently being treated abroad. Some of the bills are huge: tens of thousands of euros. Particularly those from Israeli hospitals. Lithuania and Poland are treating the injured for free. The administration of military hospitals, as well as the administration of the MVD (Ministry of Internal Affairs) hospital, refuse our aid, even though the wife of one of the injured policemen appealed to us and received money to buy essential medicine. Two *berkutovtsy* are still in intensive care at the MVD hospital, in a coma, one of them with two bullets in his head. But the administration says they have all they need to care for these men.

There have also been victims from the pro-Russian demonstrations in Donetsk, Kharkiv and Luhansk, and they are asking us for support. Of the 3,129,000 hryvnas collected by the foundation, we have already spent nearly half. Financial aid and medical care have already been given to 158 people. Fifty-six patients have left hospital, for the moment, their medical bills paid in full. However, there are problems that the foundation cannot resolve on its own. A 51-year-old Afghan, Valeriy Fisun, received payment for the treatment of a damaged eye and spinal injuries, but his identity papers remained at his home in Crimea. He can't return for them, because the police have already been looking for him several times at his address. For now, he is living in a tent in the Maidan. What will happen to him when the Maidan is taken down? Who will take care of a case like his? The problem now is to find him a new place to live and to establish an ID for him.

As I was walking home from the foundation meeting, on the corner of Reitarskaya Street and Vladimirskaya Street, near the fish restaurant, a man dressed in camouflage suddenly appeared in front of me. His jacket was half open, offering a glimpse of the flashing blade of a machete, which I could see was attached to his belt. He was walking steadily and confidently, as if he knew exactly where he was going. The look on his young face was tough and expressionless, giving him the appearance of a cross between a young Che Guevara and a patient from a psychiatric hospital. I briefly thought about stopping him and saying: 'Excuse me, brother, but which *sotnya* are you from?' I didn't, though. Firstly because he was walking too fast and clearly had no intention of stopping to talk with an unknown civilian. Secondly, the icy gleam of that steel blade was threatening. And thirdly, my question might have seemed provocative to him, because there was nothing on his clothing that suggested he belonged to any of the Maidan's self-defence *sotnyas*.

There are some strange people mixed up in the revolution these days. Some of them are simple criminals or ex-cons who, under the cover of Pravy Sektor, pillage shops and farm cooperatives in the south of Ukraine. In the Dnipropetrovsk region, special detachments of police capture half a dozen false Pravy Sektor groups every day, all of them devoted to theft in local villages and hamlets. Special detachments resident in the big cooperatives have been set up so they are as close as possible to the places where crimes are likely to be committed. And, for the moment, among the two hundred or so criminals arrested while wearing camouflage and carrying a gun, not one actual member of Pravy Sektor has been found.

Saturday 5 April

Gabriela's birthday: she is seventeen today. A sunny morning, and the rest of the day promises more of the same. We agreed to give her 1,200 hryvnas for her cake and party meal. Today, for the first time, she will go on a training course to learn how to be a radio presenter – perhaps this way she will come up with some more substantial ideas about her future, or at least she will know what she definitely doesn't want to do. She is inviting friends to our apartment after the meal and they will party until dawn. She asked our advice about creating a programme of activities. We suggested a karaoke competition and various games. All I asked is that she and her friends do not go out onto the balcony or sit on the guardrail. We are on the third floor, after all, and Aleksey, who lives below us, has told me several times that he has seen my daughter sitting on the balcony railing.

Yesterday, Pravy Sektor declared, out of the blue, that 5 April ('Volunteer Saturday') would be devoted to dismantling the barricades in the centre of Kiev. Kievites began to get ready. But in the evening, the party's representatives made a correction: due to a 'human factor', there had been an error and Saturday would not be the day the barricades were dismantled, but the earlier order was redirected to the area around the barricades and a clean-up of the refuse and litter that clutter it. The barricades would remain at least until the presidential elections on 25 May, since the revolution was not over and the Maidan was the sole force capable of controlling the interim government and its actions.

Volunteer Saturday did take place today. The city sent several trucks, and Maidanistas and Kievites spent half the day loading them with rubbish. Many people brought their entire families, including very young chidren, and I heard those kids, still too young to go to school, loudly discussing Russia's occupation of Crimea, all the while helping their parents tidy up. I imagine that these events will soon enter the history books.

But I fear that those same history books will also contain events that have not yet taken place. The tension persists, particularly due to a worsening crime situation that has now extended into Kiev. Last week, in the lobby of a building on Semirenko Street, where my parents live, criminals robbed a family, having first savagely beaten the father, a businessman in his fifties, who died in hospital of a haemorrhage. At 8 Nekrasov Street, not far from where we live, four apartments were burgled in the space of a single day. Now, Liza and I remind the children every day not to open the door to strangers, no matter what they say. Even if they claim to have come to read the gas meter or deliver a registered letter, the children must not open the door to them. It is, quite simply, dangerous.

In the east of Ukraine, close to the Russian border, the troubles continue. Today, almost six hundred pro-Russian activists marched in Donetsk for half the day, waving Russian flags and demanding a referendum. In Mariupol, a large industrial city on the Sea of Azov, pro-Russian militants stormed the City Prosecutor's building and pillaged it. Police did not arrest anyone, but the chief of police said they were watching the situation and had identified the culprits. They plan to arrest the leaders and activists later. That 'later' is a little frightening. On Friday, in the same region, agents from Ukraine's security services apprehended fifteen Russian citizens who had illegally smuggled in three hundred Kalashnikovs, a grenade launcher and a load of other military equipment. The weapons were confiscated, the commando unit imprisoned.

Russia immediately announced that twenty-five members of Pravy Sektor had been arrested in Moscow because they were planning an attack. Afterwards it was revealed that all those prisoners were immigrant construction workers, originally from Zakarpattya, in western Ukraine. Not that the Russians care: as far as they are concerned, the men are simply Ukrainian extremists because they speak Ukrainian to one another.

The war is also being carried out on another front. At the end of last week, on Friday, in Cherkasy, not far from Kiev, the journalist and Maidan activist Vasiliy Sergienko was kidnapped, tortured and killed by unknown hands.

In Crimea, the inhabitants have until 18 April to report to one of the four emigration centres and sign a declaration refusing Russian nationality. If they do not do so, they will, from 18 April, automatically be considered Russian citizens. If they do sign, they will be considered foreigners and must leave the peninsula within ninety days. They may also go through the formalities required to obtain a residence permit for foreigners, in compliance with Russian Federation law. For the moment, though, the emigration centres – which are not spread all over Crimea but are all located close to Simferopol – are not registering declarations of refusal of Russian nationality, but simply noting down those who wish to remain Ukrainian citizens on a special list. What will they do with this list afterwards? No one knows. What is certain is that remaining a Ukrainian citizen in occupied Crimea will be complicated and possibly dangerous. Despite the fact that Russia accepts dual nationality, that right does not exist for Crimeans. As soon as they ask for a Russian passport, they must make a written renunciation of Ukrainian nationality.

We arrived in Lazarevka this evening – Liza, Theo, Anton and me. It was another two hours before the sun set. Our neighbour Tolya gave us four buckets of tiny potatoes, which Anton, Theo and

I set to work planting in the garden. We worked until nightfall. We will finish the job tomorrow morning.

We had brought a wok with us, and I made a turkey, vegetable and noodle stir-fry for dinner, with a spicy Chinese sauce. But we didn't bring anything from Kiev for dessert, unfortunately.

Sunday 6 April

A cold but sunny morning.

Invigorated by the cool air, the cockerels of Lazarevka crowed earlier than usual. But I was already up, having woken at six. We continued planting potatoes. Just as we had finished the fourth patch of the vegetable garden, our neighbour, Father Petro, came to tell us that he wanted to give us another sack of potatoes to plant. We didn't have enough time left to put them in the earth, so we took them down to the cellar. We will deal with them in a couple of weeks, before Easter.

Russian media announced today that a rally was held in Alchevsk. About 160 activists, of uncertain sobriety, gathered for this demonstration, known as 'Russian Spring', to demand the nationalisation of something or other, as well as more social justice. Then they flew the French flag. Clearly they are not very sure what the Russian flag actually looks like, but at least they got the colours right. After that, they all went home.

A complete list has appeared on the Internet, detailing the *efesbeshniki* (FSB agents), *grushniki* (GRU agents, the Main Intelligence Directorate of the Russian Federation) and other specialists in shady business who were staying in Kiev at the time of the Maidan shootings. Some were living in the offices of the SBU, in Kontsa-Zaspa, the others in a hotel. Lots of generals and colonels among them. About forty or fifty in total. Sergey Lavrov, Russia's Foreign Affairs Minister, explained that all these intelligence officers and other specialists in popular uprisings

– including expert consultants from Transnistria, Abkhazia and South Ossetia – were in Kiev to protect the Russian embassy. And yet none of them were staying in their home embassy, and most of them did not even visit it.

Monday 7 April

I dropped the children at school this morning, then went straight to see my mum. I took her to hospital for a cardiogram and blood tests. We spent two hours there. Then I dropped her back at her apartment, went home myself, and settled down to work. I worked until evening, pausing only to check the news.

The Printemps Français Festival opened this evening at the Premier Palace Hotel. This annual celebration of French art and literature, organised each spring by the French embassy, is now in its eleventh year. I went with Liza. We met lots of old film-making friends. We chatted with Eric Tosatti, director of the French Institute in Kiev, and with the French and German ambassadors. They are all coming to our apartment tomorrow for wine and cheese, along with French writers who are here for the festival and their Ukrainian counterparts. I definitely need to buy more wine.

The fourth Arsenal International Book Festival begins tomorrow, when the French ambassador will award me the Legion of Honour. Difficult to guess how much wine we might drink to celebrate that. Particularly when most of the guests are French!

Tuesday 8 April

The morning drizzle has given way to sunshine. Our first-floor neighbours are still renovating their apartment; through the open balcony window, I hear the whine of a drill.

In the newspaper, no news of Luhansk, where the separatists and their Russian colleagues have seized the SBU building and, consequently, are in possession of the weapons that had previously been taken from them, as well as all those belonging to Ukraine's security services. But yesterday, in the east, the anti-terrorist operation finally began. In Kharkiv, for the second time in two days, separatists were flushed out of the regional administration building and the local television building. Seventy people were arrested, but they will probably all be released soon.

In Donetsk, the separatists are still laying siege to the SBU. Although the separatists are armed, they are negotiating, at least since yesterday, and the outcome is uncertain. Rinat Akhmetov went to meet them, which leads one to think that he is well informed about what is happening. He chose a few people to lead negotiations with the authorities and stated his support for the protesters if the attack was mounted against the occupied building, and said he would be 'with the people'. One of the combatants asked him: 'And who should we vote for?' and he replied: 'For the Party of Regions. It will be on the ballot. I'm a member too.' In Mykolaiv, a peaceful mafia town of drug addicts and medium-sized companies, there was an attempt to seize the general administration, but only a few dozen people took part. The assault was defeated by citizens who gathered to defend the building. Result: ten wounded, and one of the defenders was shot. Later, police seized dozens of clubs, pistols and a rifle from the separatists' tents. In Dnipropetrovsk, there was no attack; in Odessa, separatists marched on the administration building, but changed their minds before they got there. Also yesterday, a Russian GRU agent was arrested: Roman Bannykh was coordinating the actions of separatists in Donestk and Luhansk, by telephone. The SBU published his telephone conversations with those separatists on the Internet.

The interim Foreign Minister, Andriy Deshchytsya, spoke on the phone with his Russian counterpart Sergey Lavrov, who is demanding that no one attacks the separatists, and that authorities respond to their 'legitimate demands'!

In the meantime, Kiev has agreed to accept Ukrainian prisoners held up to now in Crimean prisons, while Russia promised to cure Crimean drug addicts in its own hospitals. As the peninsula's inhabitants continue to struggle with their problems in obtaining a Russian passport, more than three hundred Soviet monuments in Crimea have changed nationality. Most of the monuments are connected to the Second World War. It seems that, for Russia, the establishment of a passport for a monument is more important than for a mere citizen. This is understandable: there are few citizens who become monuments, whereas the monuments are already in place, sitting proudly atop their pedestals, and will remain there for a long time, if not forever.

Wednesday 9 April

Yesterday, while I was on my way to a meeting, Natasha Kolomoytseva called me on my mobile. She told me that she had been walking on the banks of the Dnieper, not far from the Rusanovka embankment where she lives, when she saw a car stop in front of the floating hotel-restaurant and people taking weapons from the vehicle to the hotel. She was scared and wondered what to do. She took down the car's registration number. I advised her to call the SBU or the police. Soon afterwards she called me back to say that no one was answering any of the various numbers for the SBU she had found on the Internet, but that the police had promised to send a patrol car. Then the police had turned up at her house and behaved strangely. They said they hadn't found anything suspicious, took her mobile phone number, and told her that a local officer would be round to see her. Now she was worried by the idea that the police might pass the details on to some other department. I looked up the number for Ihor Smeshko, head of the SBU from 2003 to 2005. I didn't manage to get hold of him at home, but I sent him all the information on Facebook, including the car's registration number. That evening, he replied to say he had sent the information to be verified. Phew! I hope this case is now being handled by professionals.

Last night, while we were opening the book festival and I was receiving the Legion of Honour from Alain Rémy, the French ambassador to Ukraine, in Luhansk the situation continued to worsen around the SBU's regional government building.

The occupying separatists have nearly a thousand guns, lots of Kalashnikovs and even grenade launchers. They have taken more than fifty hostages. The separatists are in constant communication with Russia, from where these actions are being coordinated. The men inside the occupied building also communicate by phone with their supporters in the Luhansk region. The security services are spying on some of these conversations, and what they heard makes it clear that during the night, at 5 a.m., Russian troops were readying to enter Ukrainian territory. The Russian coordinators asked the separatists to neutralise the border guards on a country road, so that their soldiers could enter Ukraine and, as planned, support the besieged separatists in Luhansk.

In spite of the concentration of troops observed in the Luhansk region, however, the Russian army did not cross the Ukrainian border. It was probably prevented from doing so by the fact that the Ukrainian border guards have been reinforced with military units transferred from other regions. Nevertheless, the attack could occur at any time. Television cameras recorded a brief harangue recalling old Hollywood Z-movies. The central message, delivered by several men in balaclavas and camouflage outfits, bedecked with various weapons, was this: 'Welcome to Hell!' For the moment, negotiations seem to be going nowhere. But most of the hostages – security service agents – have been released. I fear this situation will inevitably end in bloodshed.

In Donetsk, on the other hand, things have improved a little. The men who had taken over the regional SBU building have left, without their weapons. The regional administration building is still occupied, though, surrounded by barricades and piles of tyres, which the separatists set on fire from time to time. They claim to have a vast stock of Molotov cocktails. In Mykolaiv, everything has calmed down, and in Odessa too, apparently.

In Crimea, a Russian sergeant shot an unarmed Ukrainian major who needed to cross into continental Ukraine to continue his military service. He was buried today in Berdyansk, while the man reportedly responsible for his death, Sergeant Zaytsev, has not even been charged. He is still at large. It won't be long before killing someone in Crimea because they don't want a Russian passport is not even considered a crime.

How vast my country seems. Here in Kiev, I have the impression that all this is happening on the other side of the world!

We celebrated my Legion of Honour at home yesterday, and the party went on until nearly midnight. My two cousins were there with their families, and so were the Kapranov brothers, my three editors, the French and German ambassadors, French diplomats and writers here for the book festival, and other friends. We spent almost the whole evening talking about the Maidan, describing what each of us had been through.

Thursday 10 April

The pro-Russian paramilitary mess continues in Ukraine. The deadline for the ultimatum is up, apparently. The occupiers of the Luhansk SBU building have been promised amnesty, as well as exemption from punishment for storming the building and stealing weapons. There can be no doubt that they have other weapons. So, if they disperse now after the amnesty, it will only be to regather somewhere else and start again. We need to photograph them, list their names, create a database so that we know in detail who Putin's agents are, where they live and what they look like. The blockade of military bases continues, as does the presidential campaign. The main pro-Russian candidate was unexpectedly punched in the face yesterday in the southern town of Mykolaiv, his designer suit sprayed with *zelenka* by hostile locals who also insulted him as a spy in the pay of Russia. The official Party of Regions candidate, Dobkin, had a similarly unpleasant time, also in the south-east, where he was sprayed with mayonnaise. At our age, of course, mayonnaise is terribly harmful, as it increases cholesterol levels in the blood.

Sunday 13 April

The anti-terrorist operation began secretly and somewhat confusedly. There were bursts of gunfire on both roads into Slovyansk, in the Donetsk region, and one SBU agent was killed by separatists, with another five injured, among them the deputy leader of the special Alpha SBU detachment. Russia is making threats again. Lavrov is demanding that Ukraine stops using weapons against the armed separatists who have seized local government, police and SBU buildings, and who are themselves firing at the police! Ukraine, it is true, remained silent when Russia went to war, a few years ago, with Chechen separatists, sometimes also killing representatives of the civilian population.

Good news for Crimean prisoners. The possibility of offering amnesty to those who wish to obtain Russian nationality is now being examined. Those who do not want a Russian passport will probably be sent to continental Ukraine to continue serving their sentences.

Monday 14 April

Although the population of Slovyansk was warned this morning not to take their children to school, it is now midday and nothing has happened. The separatists are still in the same places and are even being reinforced. Turchynov, the interim president, is dragging his heels. He doesn't want to be held responsible for a shootout that, if it occurs, will be long and noisy.

He mentioned earlier today the possibility of organising a referendum on Ukraine's integrity at the same time as the 25 May presidential elections. A completely intelligent idea. But an idea that will not suit Russia, which would then have to end the war on Ukrainian territory.

We ate dinner as a family this evening, and even Gabriela did not go out afterwards to join her friends at the cafe. The reason for this turned out to be very serious: she wanted to talk with me about inflation. She spoke coherently, and for quite a long time, before concluding, as I expected, with a request for an increase in her weekly pocket money, because the cost of living had gone up since the crisis began. So, all right, we'll increase it.

Tuesday 15 April

It is raining. Russia continues to lose its mind. In a children's theatre in Moscow, the staging of Gianni Rodari's work *Cipollino* has been hurriedly reworked. The story of the vegetables' revolution against Prince Lemon has been deleted. In its place, in a new variation, the discontented vegetables present Prince Lemon with a petition demanding reforms. And Lyudmila's solo has been scrapped from Glinka's opera *Ruslan and Lyudmila* – part of the programme of concerts for Moscow's Historical and Cultural Heritage Days – on the basis that the text included the words 'Dnieper' and 'Kiev'.

The writer and journalist Zhenya Polozhiy, the editor of the regional newspaper *Panorama*, was violently attacked late this evening, in Sumy, in the north-east of Ukraine. He has an open fracture in his arm. He had managed to avoid the worst during the Maidan rebellion in Sumy, of which he was one of the organisers. But now that the Maidan has won and the struggle for Ukraine's integrity has begun, pro-European activists and journalists are being attacked in various towns by unknown hands.

My old friend Tanya told me today that her neighbour, a single woman of thirty-nine, had hidden two wounded protesters during the Maidan rebellion. One of them, a chef in a Lviv restaurant, had been shot three times in the leg; the other, also from Lviv, had been beaten so badly by Berkut agents that he was unrecognisable. His nose was broken, one ear torn, his jaw damaged. Automaidan activists brought volunteer doctors to provide first aid. Then, in the middle of the night, they fetched a surgeon and converted one of the apartment's rooms into an operating theatre. The three bullets were removed from the cook's leg. One day, when the woman came home from work, the wounded chef apologised to her: he had been through her freezer without her permission. There, he had found a chicken, which he had thawed and cooked for her as an expression of his gratitude.

Wednesday 16 April

The rain seems to be abating. Milder weather is forecast for the next few days. This is good news, as we intend to go to the countryside for Easter.

In the east, all is calm, after yesterday's battle for the military airfield in the Donetsk region. Or, at least, no information is getting through. More taped conversations involving separatists – talking to each other, and to Moscow – have been published online by the SBU. The name Yevgeniy Fyodorov keeps coming up. This State Duma deputy became famous by declaring that the late Russian rock star, Viktor Tsoy, collaborated with the CIA during the Soviet era, and that the American secret services, assisted by Hollywood professionals, wrote songs for him aimed at causing the decadence and ruin of the Soviet Union. In the mind of Fyodorov, the song most responsible for triggering the collapse of the USSR was entitled 'We Demand Changes'.

On the road out of Crimea, border guards arrested four young people – one boy and three girls – who were transporting money for Donbas: wages or financial aid intended for the separatists, almost two million hryvnas in total.

Russian television showed images of a helicopter hit by rocket-launcher fire, claiming that the separatists were shooting down Ukrainian helicopters and aeroplanes. This video has been shown for the past month, and it turns out that it was actually shot in Syria, near Aleppo. According to Russia, the number of separatists killed varies between four and thirty, but the Ukrainian authorities say there have been no fatalities and dozens of arrests. There has certainly not been any video footage or photographs of the Kramatorsk airfield after the fighting that showed any dead or wounded.

There was a confrontation yesterday, outside the courthouse in Kiev, between Pravy Sektor and former Berkut members who had come to support their colleague, arrested for having shot at protesters in the Maidan. The Pravy Sektor activists surrounded the *berkutovtsy* and demanded that they get down on their knees and ask the Ukrainian people for forgiveness. They apologised but refused to kneel. The incident ended peacefully: the Pravy Sektor members agreed with the Berkut agents that they would all go to the east of Ukraine together to defend the state's integrity. Just like a Hollywood happy ending.

Thursday 17 April

In Luhansk, separatists have taken a journalist hostage. Ukraine has closed its borders to all single men aged between sixteen and sixty with a Russian passport or who are resident in Crimea. Russia has sworn to retaliate 'in an appropriate way'. The day began with the prohibition on imported Ukrainian salami and the promise that a similar ban on cheese will soon follow.

I drove my car to the Mitsubishi garage for its regular service. After leaving it there, I walked towards the Podil market, thinking of buying some freshly baked *lavash*, and some *suluguni* cheese sold by a Georgian stallholder I know. I had no hryvnas in my pockets, only euros. I tried changing the money in three banks, but none of them changed currencies. I have had problems with this for the last three days. Either the banks don't have any hryvnas or their computers are down. The hryvna is rising at the moment, while the euro falls. The National Bank penalised fourteen different banks for currency speculation. So I wasn't able to buy anything from the Podil market.

I went with Theo and Anton to the Theatre of Russian Drama. We saw a new show there about Taras Shevchenko, *Everywhere Alone*. There were two Shevchenkos onstage: a young Russian-speaking one, and an older Ukrainian-speaking one with a long, drooping white moustache. The play was bilingual. Some actors spoke Ukrainian, others Russian. This is an amusing idea, but the first part proved a little dull, and the boys were not thrilled by the play. On the way home, I noticed three new Rolls-Royce cars in the windows of a dealership in the Leonardo Business Centre. No one imports cars like that to a country on the verge of war. Does someone have inside information that the war won't happen?

And, as if in confirmation, an agreement for 'de-escalation' was announced today after negotiations in Geneva. Lavrov signed too. Admittedly, Putin answered questions in Russia today, and not once did he mention the word 'de-escalation'. On the contrary, he reminded journalists that he had a mandate from the Federation Council to use troops in Ukraine. But I feel a little more serene at the moment. I want to believe that no one will be killed tonight in the east of the country.

In Donetsk and other cities, there were rallies in support of a united Ukraine. In Kramatorsk, separatists attacked the pro-Ukrainian demonstration, but the police restored order and no one was injured.

Putin has again demanded that the Ukrainian army not use force against the peaceful pro-Russian activists who walk around in combat uniform, with no badges or other signs of identification, carrying AK-100 assault rifles. The Ukrainian army does not possess those rifles, but the Russian army does. According to the SBU, of the 117 Russian citizens arrested for having taken part in disturbances, at least ten are Russian secret service agents. Lavrov and Putin maintain that not a single Russian officer is in Ukrainian territory. Really? – and what about in Crimea?

Sunday 20 April

Lazarevka. Theo and I finished planting the potatoes yesterday. Liza made the dough for the *paskhas*. She made five of them – two big ones and three small ones, as the tradition is that there should be one for each family member. The sky hazy, but luminous.

Not a sound this morning. The whole village is asleep. But at 3 a.m., dozens of villagers passed silently in front of the house, holding lit candles, carrying baskets that contained the *paskhas* and the painted eggs. They went to the church, where the Easter service has been going on since yesterday evening. But only a brave few usually attend the entire service; the others gather around the church and wait, with their baskets at their feet, for the priest to come out and bless the parishioners and everything they have brought with them. When we went to the church last year, we noticed home-made salami and bottles of vodka or schnapps in many of the baskets, barely concealed behind the eggs and the bread.

After lunch, all the people in the village began to visit one another. We were invited by our neighbours. Then we went to the Maystruks', where we spent almost two hours talking, eating and sipping Metaxa.

Monday 21 April

During the night before Easter – from Saturday night to Sunday morning – a 'paschal miracle' occurred in the city of Slovyansk. A group of supposedly peaceful, unarmed citizens, representatives of the separatists who were guarding a checkpoint on the road that leads into the city, repelled an attack by a large gang of combatants who arrived in four Jeeps, riddling two of the enemy's vehicles with bullets and reducing them to ashes. But the miracle was not that unarmed citizens were able to riddle their attackers with bullets, but that – in the middle of the soot and ashes of the burnt-out vehicles – they found, untouched by the flames, several brand-new $100 bills and business cards belonging to the Pravy Sektor leader, Dmytro Yarosh. Impossible not to think instantly of the biblical legend of the burning bush. No, not everything burns in the flames of this Ukrainian conflict.

But that was not the only miracle in Slovyansk. The separatists, who refused to speak to Ukrainian journalists, told Russian television that there had been three deaths on their side and 'up to seven' on the enemy's side. However, said the unarmed citizens, the nationalists had taken their dead and wounded away in the remaining cars. An examination of the scene of the alleged battle did not reveal any traces of blood, and the only known victim turns out to be an inhabitant of a neighbouring village who was going home in his car and seems to have been killed by the defenders of the checkpoint themselves. The other inhabitants of that village are convinced that their neighbour was killed before the supposed battle, in order for his body to be shown on Russian television. As for the defenders of the checkpoint who fell under the attackers' bullets...not a word! Which leads me to think that if any people really were killed during this confrontation, they must have been Russian citizens rather than natives. Otherwise their families would already have recovered their bodies and would be busy preparing their funerals, a public ceremony that is not concealed from the community.

Yes, miracles always seem to occur when there are major religious holidays. In fact, Russia promised one to Ukraine: several Russian politicians, along with the self-proclaimed prime minister of Crimea, Aksyonov, announced during the night before Easter that the former Ukrainian president, Viktor Yanukovych, would make an appearance in the region of Donbas. The whole of Ukraine went into shock. Journalists began fantasising about his itinerary: how and where would he enter Ukrainian territory? The majority came to the conclusion that Russian soldiers would take him secretly at night to the Ukrainian coast of the Sea of Azov and hand him over to his supporters in Donbas, who would take him straight to the monastery in Slavyanogorsk, close to Slovyansk, and from there, holding an icon in his hands, he would lead his loyal followers in an attack on the capital. This miracle did not actually occur, however, and by Monday the aforementioned leader of Crimea, Aksyonov – already confirmed by Vladimir Putin as a top-level Russian government employee – declared on Twitter that Yanukovych had chickened out this time, but that he would appear in Donbas on 11 May.

This promise, accompanied by the exact date of Yanukovych's next arrival in his native land, provides us with a clearer understanding of Russia's plans for the near future. On 9 May, Russia and Ukraine will celebrate the Day of Victory over Nazi Germany. Usually, Russian and pro-Russian forces, including the communists, take advantage of this anniversary to engage in provocations. The communists march under the flag of the USSR, waving red pennants, which immediately attracts the attention of Ukrainian nationalists and all other enemies of communism and the Soviet past. A past that is still deeply embedded in the hearts and minds of many inhabitants of Donbas. The Day of Victory demonstrations are liable – with the support of a few stage directors, Russian or native – to turn into riots, and into further attacks on administrative buildings, police stations, army barracks and security service headquarters. And then, at the crucial moment, the saviour of Donbas – Viktor Yanukovych – will appear.

It is obvious that Yanukovych himself has no desire to return to Ukraine, which means that all the operations involving his possible participation are being planned by the Russian secret services. They are eager to play the Yanukovych card before the Ukrainian presidential elections. Once those elections are over, Russia will have no further need for Yanukovych.

Meanwhile, in Slovyansk, which is entirely under the control of separatists, several houses belonging to gypsies have been pillaged. Separatist representatives have stated that these pogroms were legitimate as the houses' owners, suspected of drug dealing, were searched at the same time. Similarly legitimate is the fact that two Ukrainian journalists have been taken hostage and that the former mayor of Slovyansk, Nelya Shtepa – who supported the separatists to begin with but then stood up to them because she said they were being manipulated by Russian secret service agents – has been illegally confined in an unknown location.

The television transmitter in Slovyansk has also been seized by separatists. None of the Ukrainian channels are on air any more, while all the Russian ones work perfectly. And a new Slovyansk channel has begun broadcasting, wasting no time in announcing that the government in Kiev is run by Jews.

In the neighbouring city of Luhansk, the separatists who seized the SBU building are no longer talking about a People's Republic of Donetsk which would also include the Luhansk region, but about an autonomous Luhanskian republic. Clearly, their hopes of military aid from Russia are dwindling.

And while part of eastern Ukraine's territories remain under the control of pro-Russian forces, the governor of the Dnipropetrovsk region, the oligarch Ihor Kolomoyskyi, has promised a $10,000 reward for each captured Russian soldier. As the owner of Privatbank, the largest bank in Ukraine, he has already sent $50,000 and a detachment of Ukrainian parachutists to successfully repel a separatist attack in the Donetsk region. Previous presidents' promises to professionalise the Ukrainian army remained wishful thinking, but now that one of the richest men in the country has paid the soldiers in cold, hard cash for accomplishing their first duties, the professional army is in the process of becoming a reality. It is, of course, regrettable that the country's army is dependent for its existence on wealthy sponsors.

Tuesday 22 April

I dropped the boys at school this morning. On the way, Theo asked: 'Dad, who was better, Stalin or Lenin?' Lenin, I replied, because he died younger! The boys agreed, satisfied by this answer.

In Russia, the authorities have finally revealed both sides of the medal 'for the reintegration of Crimea', awarded to those anonymous heroes of the Russian army who took part in the occupation of the peninsula. Putin even said: 'You won't know their names, but they will be decorated!' The most interesting detail is the fact that the dates of the operation to annex Crimea are engraved on the medals: '20-02-2014–18-03-2014'. In other words, Russia began this operation while Yanukovych was still in Kiev, before he started planning to flee, before the protesters in the Maidan were massacred. And so the secret is revealed.

Mykola Kravchenko, one of my publishers, took me to Cherkasy for the day. It's a nice town, 140 miles from Kiev, situated on the Dnieper River. The police had closed the Pereyaslav-Khmelnytskyi ring road. Later, we learned that, half an hour before we got there, a service station had exploded, destroying the little shop and cafe. On the radio, the suspicion was immediately of a terrorist attack, but in fact it turned out to be a simple gas explosion. Six people died; seven were injured and have been hospitalised. When we crossed the bridge over the Dnieper, there was a checkpoint on the other side, set up by armed policemen and soldiers. We waved at them and continued on our way.* The tension persists, and even though Donetsk is over six hundred miles away from Cherkasy, people still live in fear of terrorist attacks.

In Cherkasy, I met students from the technical institute, then I gave speeches at the regional library and the fine arts museum. We went back to Kiev around midnight, listening to the news all the way home. The Pereyaslav-Khmelnytskyi ring road was still closed, so we had to make a detour.

---

* The author's car was not checked because it had a Kiev number plate.

Thursday 24 April

A sunny day. The morning began with a telephone call from a friend who exports Ukrainian books to Russia. 'Congratulations!' he said. I thought he was wishing me a happy birthday. But in fact he was congratulating me on the fact that my novel *The President's Last Love* had been banned in Russia. Of course, he added, I would now have to send a copy of the book to the Russian Federal Agency of Press and Mass Communications so that it could assess the presence of extremist propaganda or other elements liable to harm the Russian Federation. According to Russian law, the assessment must take place within two months of receiving the book. In two months' time, I hope to receive a copy of the agency's conclusions!

My guests left early last night, about 11 p.m. It was a good party. Towards the end, I played a little piano and sang two or three songs. After that, I felt hoarse, so I kept my mouth shut for the rest of the evening. The presents remain as a souvenir of my birthday party: five bottles of whisky, one of cognac, a painting and a hammock for our country house. When the boys opened the parcel containing the hammock this morning, they were thrilled. And straight away they started fighting over who would be the first one to try it when we found a place for it in Lazarevka.

The situation in Ukraine is relatively calm today. In spite of the Foreign Minister Lavrov's threats, the Russian army has not crossed the Ukrainian border. Some separatists fired at police helicopters, while others attempted to storm the military base in Artemivsk, but the soldiers managed to repel them. In Mariupol, a group armed with clubs attacked the separatists who were occupying the mayor's office and chased them from the building. Kiev's interim mayor announced that there would no longer be a New Year tree in the Maidan. Another place would be found for it, in the centre of the city, and the Maidan would remain a place of remembrance for those who died during the protests.

The Festival of Ukrainian Literature opens today in Donetsk, while dozens of Russian writers, critics and intellectuals arrive in Kiev for the conference organised by Mikhail Khodorkovsky.

A debate is going on in Crimea about Putin's bill approving the opening of a special gambling zone in the peninsula. The idea of transforming Crimea into a huge casino does not please the Tatars nor the inhabitants of Sevastopol, who were hoping Moscow would turn them into a new Silicon Valley.

Ukrainian troops have regained control of the small town of Slavyanogorsk, not far from Slovyansk which had been seized by separatists. We are now anxiously awaiting 9 May. If Ukraine survives the Day of Victory, the chances of proceeding to the presidential elections and restoring some stability will be increased.

This evening, Liza and I discuss how best to help Theo pass his exams in June. I realise with surprise that the school exams will begin one week after the presidential elections, set for 25 May. There is no doubt that the exams will take place. But what about the elections? I want to believe they will, but I am not sure of it.

Everyone is tired of dreading war, of hearing Russia's threats, of fearing the future. We would like to turn over this page of Ukraine's history as quickly as possible.

Afterword

I'm writing this on 27 June. President Petro Poroshenko signed an Association Agreement with the European Union today in Brussels. Also today, in an interview with the BBC, an adviser to the Russian president, Sergey Glazyev, once again referred to Poroshenko and his government as Nazis. And earlier this morning, on the final day of the ceasefire declared a week ago by the Ukrainian president, pro-Russian separatists killed another five Ukrainian soldiers and officers in the east of the country.

Since my last diary entry on 24 April, the reality of life in Ukraine has undergone a series of transformations. Despite all these changes it has remained and will continue to remain, to paraphrase the doctors, stable but critical.

Over the past two months the Ukrainian people have been introduced to the concept of 'hybrid war': an expression coined to mean war initiated in any country by a neighbouring state without mobilising their own troops but by supplying arms and volunteers to rebel insurgents in the country loyal to the neighbouring state, who believe that life is better there. The neighbouring state – in this case Russia – persistently denies involvement in the military situation in eastern Ukraine, but when challenged directly to explain how the separatists come to be in possession of tanks and military technology registered to the armed forces of the Russian Federation they do not reply. Russian volunteers return home – to Rostov-on-Don, Lipetsk or the suburbs of Moscow – in zinc-lined coffins, a familiar image from the war in Afghanistan. Another reminder of Afghanistan is the resurrection of the expression 'Cargo 200' – the military term for dead soldiers being transported back to their homeland. The expression 'Cargo 300' also exists and is used to refer to the wounded. But Russia does not welcome her wounded soldiers home. If truth be told, she would rather not accept her dead citizens either. With the exception of the opposition newspaper *Novaya Gazeta*, the Russian press does not even mention the Russian death toll in Ukraine. The funerals of these soldiers are conducted in virtual secrecy too, under the supervision of Russia's FSB. Russian nationalists complain on social networking sites that no one is writing about those who are dying for the 'Russian idea', that they are not being honoured. The fact is that no one knows exactly how many Russian volunteers are fighting in Ukraine or how many have already died. And we probably never will. All we know is the number of Ukrainian soldiers and civilians who have lost their lives.

But the war is confined to one region, representing a relatively small proportion of the overall territory of Ukraine. In Kiev, life has returned to normal. Lviv recently hosted the international Alfa Jazz Fest, and the city of Konotop, not far from the Russian border, held its annual festival celebrating local military history. The 2014 Odessa International Film Festival is expected to go ahead as planned, and writers and publishers are currently preparing for the largest book fair in Ukraine, which will take place in September also in the charming city of Lviv – the cultural capital of Ukraine, a city every bit as beautiful and stylish as Paris or Vienna.

I still haven't resumed work on my Lithuanian novel, but I have every hope of sitting down to it in the coming weeks. The past six months have deeply affected the Ukrainian psyche. Even I feel as though my sense of humour has waned, and I'm not sure when I'll fully regain control over my emotions. Sometimes when I'm arguing in silence with people who disagree with me on Facebook, I suddenly feel like shouting out loud, telling them to switch to

Skype so that we can look one another in the eye and speak from the heart. Fortunately, I've managed to stop myself so far. People don't listen to one another during wartime.

Meanwhile, the Maidan, our European revolution, has become history. But this history is unfinished, not yet ready to be a page in a textbook. Of course ex-President Yanukovych is currently living in Russia, and he was followed there by several dozen former members of the Cabinet and former heads of the police force and the secret services. In other words, an entire class of corrupt Ukrainian politicians (as if there were any other kind!) and civil servants have become political refugees. The country is governed by new people now, and Ukraine believes in them – for the time being. The new government has not yet launched its promised war against corruption on all levels. Admittedly, it is hard to wage war on two fronts at the same time. There is not much hope for an improvement of the situation on the Russian–Ukrainian front. There is not much hope for military victory either. To be honest, the prospects are fairly hopeless: either a full-blown war with thousands of casualties on both sides and an unlimited supply of modern weaponry for the separatists from Russia, or capitulation due to lack of military and technical support from Europe and NATO and the weakness of our own armed forces. Or agreement to Russia's annexation of Donbas. But agreement to the annexation of Donbas will inevitably lead to the gradual annexation by Russia of other regions too, with the exception of western Ukraine. This is what worries me. Perhaps that's why I prefer not to think about it.

I wasn't sure whether or not the presidential elections would take place in May, but I knew no one would interfere with the school exams. Theo has finished his exams now and is on holiday. The potatoes I planted near our country house have already finished flowering. I sowed courgette and pumpkin seeds too, but they didn't seem to germinate very well. Frankly, I'm not expecting a great harvest, but that doesn't matter because my neighbour Anatoliy has an impressive crop and he always gives me some. At least I'll have my own potatoes. They'll need digging up in September, regardless of the military situation. Where will I be? Where will my wife and children be in September? I want to believe that we'll be at home in Kiev, going to our country house every weekend like we usually do – grilling shashlik, gathering the harvest, making apple jam and spending the evenings in the summerhouse with a glass of wine, talking about the future. It's funny, but the future we talk about never seems to come. For some time now my wife and I have been talking more about our children's future than about our own. It makes sense, really – they have more years ahead of them than we have behind us. My wife and I already have a lot of past behind us. We're both fifty-three – we've done a lot of travelling, worked hard, lived through a great deal.

There's a Ukrainian proverb that I often hear: 'If you want to make God laugh, tell him your plans!' As far as I'm aware God doesn't read books, so I'll tell you, my readers, my plans instead. And then, in a year or so's time, I'll look back and see whether or not they came to fruition. You can check too, if you feel like it: did I make God laugh? I want to finish my Lithuanian novel by the summer of 2015, but before then I'm heading to the Frankfurt Book Fair this October, then I'm going to try and make it to the Salon du Livre in Paris in March, and in May I'm off to Georgia, where I've only been once before – in 1977! These are my personal plans. I'm not going to say anything about our family plans, as I prefer to keep them private.

Having said that, the recent events in Ukraine have certainly influenced our family life, even the way our children spend their time. From the very beginning of the Maidan, the youngest member of our family –Anton – disapproved of the way the revolutionaries were fighting with the police. As far as he was concerned the police were there to uphold law and order, which is how it should be, and in attacking them the protestors were wilfully breaking the law. Because of this hardly any of his classmates spoke to him for two weeks, and he experienced what it was like to be ostracised by his peers for his political views. As a result he developed an interest in military uniforms and started collecting items such as helmets and tunics. Kiev's most famous street, Andriyivsky Uzviz – home to Mikhail Bulgakov a hundred years ago and now one of the city's main tourist attractions – is lined with dozens of stalls selling souvenirs. You can buy all kinds of Soviet memorabilia there: red flags featuring the hammer and sickle, busts of Lenin and Stalin, every conceivable type of military uniform from the USSR. When our family was walking along Andriyivsky Uzviz recently, I noticed for the first time that the hawkers were greeting our eleven-year-old son like a close friend. He even went off for a chat with one of them, who must have been about forty. When he came back he told us gleefully that the hawker in question had managed to find a pair of Soviet leather officer's boots, to Anton's specifications – and for a good price! Not long after this, Anton came home with the boots. On arrival at our country house in Lazarevka the next day, he changed into Soviet military uniform, including a helmet and the boots, which had been polished until they gleamed, slung a gas mask over his shoulder and went out to the yard to play war. Now, I should say that Anton is fairly typical for a boy of his age – a bit lazy, not overly keen on discipline or following orders. When I told my friends about my son's new-found passion for military uniforms, they suggested that he might have read my novel *The Gardener from Ochakov*, in which the main character is transported from the present day back to the Soviet era every time he puts on an old military uniform. But I don't think Anton has read it. He's simply using his imagination, and sometimes his fantasy games involve the future. If this future is khaki-coloured it's hardly surprising, because we spend so much time discussing the key events of the war in Donbas – this strange hybrid war that we are living through.

It will come to an end at some point. Whatever the outcome, it's already quite clear that the good old Ukraine we have lived in for twenty-three years since she gained independence will no longer exist. What kind of Ukraine will replace this quiet, peaceful version, no one knows. It's easy enough to conjure up a variety of possible scenarios for the immediate future, although none of them are particularly optimistic. The main reason for this is that Europe, so vociferous in her support during the Maidan protests, has subsequently fallen silent and walked away, preferring to profit from trade with Russia. Money matters more than democracy. This cynical lesson that Europe has taught Ukraine will inevitably influence the future of my country. Which means that it will influence my own future. Ultimately, it will influence the future of Europe herself – the future of the entire European Union.

Notes

1. Yulia Tymoshenko

Yulia Volodymyrivna Tymoshenko was born in 1960 in Dnipropetrovsk, a large industrial and university city in the south-east of Ukraine, long a breeding ground for Communist Party executives. Leonid Brezhnev, the general secretary of the Communist Party of the Soviet Union from 1964 to 1982, was also from this city.

In the late 1980s, at the time of Gorbachev's economic thaw, Tymoshenko – like many other Ukrainian politicians active today – received the blessing of the All-Union Leninist Young Communist League (Komsomol) to go into business. At the time when Yulia Tymoshenko and her husband were opening a video rental store, the director of the Regional Komsomol Committeee in Dnipropetrovsk was Serhiy Tihipko – a politician and businessman, who would, by the 2004 presidential elections, be Viktor Yanukovych's campaign manager, before standing for president himself in 2010.

Yulia Tymoshenko and her husband Oleksandr rented out videos for a year. The following year, 1989, they created a youth centre called Terminal, supported by the regional committee of Komsomol. Two years later, still in conjunction with her husband, she founded the Ukrainian Petrol Corporation, which, in 1995, became the United Energy Systems of Ukraine, a financial and industrial company with a turnover of $11 billion. This company soon acquired a monopoly of the Russian gas market in Ukraine. From 1995 to 1997, Yulia

Tymoshenko was its president. In 1997, when Pavel Lazarenko – who supported and, it was thought, essentially ran the company – was dismissed from his position as prime minister, Yulia Tymoshenko gave up her presidency of the company.

After that, her career was politically rather than business oriented. On 30 December 1999, she was appointed deputy prime minister, responsible for the fuel and energy sector, in Viktor Yushchenko's government, under Leonid Kuchma's presidency.

On 19 January 2001, she was dismissed from her post, and three weeks later arrested on charges of tax fraud and smuggling Russian gas while she was running United Energy Systems of Ukraine. After forty-two days in custody, she was freed and cleared of all charges. The criminal case against her was dropped.

It was in the wake of her liberation that Yulia Tymoshenko became an active political figure and much more popular than she had been before. Using her status as a victim of Leonid Kuchma's regime, she launched a campaign – with the support of the Ukrainian Socialist and Communist parties – against President Kuchma, with the slogan *Get up, Ukraine!* She co-led the Orange Revolution in 2004, and was Prime Minister of Ukraine between January and September 2005 and again from December 2007 to March 2010. After losing the presidential election to Yanukovych, a number of criminal cases were brought against her and she was sentenced to seven years in prison. Her imprisonment was condemned by the EU and other countries and her release was a primary condition of the Association Agreement. She was released on 22 February 2014.

After three years spent in prison, her influence over political life in Ukraine has been diminished. Tymoshenko ran for president in the May 2014 elections, coming second to Petro Poroshenko.

2. Viktor Yushchenko

Viktor Yushchenko was born in 1954 in the village of Khoruzhivka, in the Sumy region, in the north-east of Ukraine. His schoolteachers remember him as a hard-working pupil, without any ambition or desire for power. After studying at the National Economic University in Ternopil, in the west of the country, he worked as an accountant in a *kolkhoz* in the Ivano-Frankivsk region, also in western Ukraine. He then did his military service as a border guard, a troop corps that reported to the KGB. After demobilising in 1976, he returned to live in the Sumy region, where he found work in the local branch of the USSR State Bank, not far from his home village. The next year, he joined the Communist Party of the Soviet Union, remaining a member until its dissolution. In 1985, he was promoted and moved to Kiev, where he continued to work for the Ukrainian branch of the USSR State Bank.

From 1993 to 1999, Viktor Yushchenko was head of the new National Bank of Ukraine, after which the second president of the Repubic, Leonid Kuchma, nominated him to be the country's prime minister. In this position, he engineered certain improvements in the banking sector and the country's economy, and began his struggle against the 'underground economy'. By doing this, he made many enemies among President Kuchma's entourage, in particular Viktor Medvedchuk, who was head of the presidential administration at the time.

In 2001, while Yulia Tymoshenko was in prison, Viktor Yushchenko signed – along with President Kuchma and the head of Parliament Ivan Plyushch – a letter addressed to the Ukrainian people in which all three described opposition representatives participating in the 'Ukraine without Kuchma' movement as fascists. However, Parliament issued a vote of no confidence in the prime minister, and his career then took on a more overtly political direction. Yushchenko presented himself as a man of the people, emphasising his love for all that is popular. He was forever showing off his collection of Ukrainian antiquities – old farming tools, *telegas,*[*] earthenware pots, and he made a big fuss about becoming a beekeeper. In the space of two years, he formed a very positive image as a popular leader who was also an economics expert. His rhetoric never appealed to Ukrainian nationalism. On the contrary: he paid far more attention to Ukraine's ancient history than to its Soviet period.

In 2002, Yushchenko's party, Our Ukraine, won the largest share of votes: almost 24 per cent. Yulia Tymoshenko's group finished second, with only 7.3 per cent. Even though the opposition forces had won, they could not manage to put together a parliamentary majority. Viktor Yushchenko, however, maintained his popularity until the presidential elections of 2004. After the victory of the Orange Revolution had made him president, he gave up politics for social issues, placing more emphasis on the cult of Holodomor and Cucuteni-Trypillian culture.

The Trypillians occupied central Ukraine five thousand years ago, and Viktor Yushchenko took pleasure in thinking that they were the ancestors of today's Ukrainians. During the early years of his presidency, the first supposedly historical works supporting this theory appeared, while new museums on Trypillian culture were inaugurated. There were also new museums on the Holodomor, dozens of monuments to the victims of the Great Famine, and the provision of funds for scientific studies on the history of that period. Films on the subject, both fictional and non-fictional, were released. This chapter was introduced into school curricula, or expanded where it already existed. The repeated emphasis on this matter provoked a lively reaction in Russia.

Prominent among Viktor Yushchenko's other ideas was creating an independent Ukrainian Orthodox Church – in other words, putting an end to the activity of the Russian Orthodox Church in Ukraine, and putting its churches under Kiev's authority. For the

---

* Wooden horse-drawn carts.

Russian Orthodox Church, which is very close to Vladimir Putin and more generally to the Russian government, such plans by the Ukrainian president were a declaration of war. This project never got past the stage of daydreams and discussions, although Ukrainian politicians do continue to mention it now and then.

On 23 August 2008, following the entry of Russian troops into Georgia, Viktor Yushchenko declared that Ukraine was going to increase its defence budget and join NATO in order to protect itself from Russia. But this declaration was not put into practice. In reality, the permanent conflict between the president and Yulia Tymoshenko's Cabinet had caused Ukraine's political evolution to grind to an almost complete standstill. A conflict with Russia over gas supplies was taking shape, and the economic situation was worsening dramatically. Viktor Yushchenko continued to accuse his prime minister, Tymoshenko, of all the world's evils, and to block every initiative she or her Cabinet came up with.

After his fiasco in the 2010 presidential elections, where he finished in fifth place with only 5.54 per cent of votes, he did all he could to ensure that Yulia Tymoshenko did not become president. He and his supporters – including various writers and other cultural figures – launched a vast propaganda campaign, aimed at encouraging people to vote 'against all candidates'* in the second round of the election. It was this vote, added to the rigging of the polls in the east and the south of Ukraine, that led to Viktor Yanukovych becoming president. Yanukovych and Yushchenko immediately bonded over their shared hatred for Yulia Tymoshenko.

Until mid-February 2014, Viktor Yushchenko continued to live in an official residence, paid for by the state: he did this with Viktor Yanukovych's permission, but in violation of the Ukrainian constitution. Only when the Euromaidan movement became more

---

* 'Against all candidates' was actually one of the voting options in the 2004 elections.

active, just before Yanukovych's escape to Russia, did Yushchenko discreetly move to his own villa near Kiev.

3. *Titushky*

This word is one of the Ukrainian language's most recent acquisitions. We even know its date of birth: 18 May 2013. It was on this day that a group of sportsmen from the small town of Bila Tserkva arrived in Kiev, each paid 250 hryvnas per day by Yanukovych's party, the Party of Regions, to provoke fights with pro-democratic protesters. The first among them to distinguish himself in these brawls was a certain Vadim Titushko, who attacked a group of reporters, knocking the female journalist Olga Snitsarchuk to the ground. This attack was filmed by other journalists, and the recordings were used as evidence during the trial. Found guilty of hindering journalistic activity and acts of violence, Vadim Titushko was initially given a prison sentence, though he was soon freed and fined 22,940 hryvnas instead. The fine was paid by representatives of the Party of Regions, who also provided the accused with a lawyer. To confuse the issue, the Party of Regions announced that Vadim Titushko was also a card-carrying journalist, which was quickly revealed to be false. It was later discovered that Titushko had previously been charged with theft and given a two-year suspended sentence. This time, he was judged at the same time as three of his comrades, members of the same martial arts club. He was given a three-year suspended sentence and ordered to pay damages and interest to his victims.

The word *titushky* appeared almost straight away. Vadim tried to go to court to ban this word, created from his surname, but without success. He has since shown support for the Maidan protests, in an attempt to rescue his public image.

Today, the term is applied to anyone hired as a mercenary by government representatives – or even by the police – to intimidate, provoke clashes or carry out violent acts against the regime's opponents. Dishonest businessmen and raiders also employ *titushky* to physically seize company offices or shops.

During Euromaidan, the *titushky* were commanded by police officers and Ukrainian security service agents.

4. Holodomor (the Great Famine of 1932–33)

This man-made famine was organised in the 1930s by the Communist Party of the Soviet Union and the government with the aim of punishing the Ukrainian peasants who did not support Stalin in his plans to collectivise the rural economy. At the time, the exportation of wheat was the Soviet Union's prime source of foreign currency. Global wheat prices had fallen, while the need for foreign money was more important than ever.

In April 1930, a law on wheat supplies was passed, according to which all *kolkhozy* (collective farms) had to hand over up to a third of their harvest to the state. This did not refer to the actual harvest, however, but the harvest required by the government for each farm. In reality, the *kolkhozy* were incapable of meeting these targets and, consequently, the state often took their entire harvest. The peasants began deserting the *kolkhozy* and moving to cities because it was impossible to survive from their work in the fields.

In Ukraine, the peasantry soon found itself in direct conflict with the government. Some *kolkhozy* refused to accept the requirements demanded by the local committees of the Communist Party, dismissing them as unrealistic. Moscow ordered a list drawn up of all the farms and peasants who were sabotaging supplies. In their districts, all deliveries of food and manufactured goods were halted. The peasants began to hoard their grain, burying it in their yards. So the government decided to recruit brigades of volunteers who would hunt for this hidden wheat. This was the beginning of the famine. Almost 110,000 peasants enrolled in these brigades, as they were given a percentage of the grain they found. Those convicted of having hidden part of their harvest were arrested and deported to Siberia. Their farms were confiscated by the Soviet government.

In January 1933, the Communist Party's Politburo approved a new supply requirement for Ukraine: 4.75 million tons. In one document, it was emphasised that this requirement must be met at any price. The result was immediate: Ukrainian peasants found themselves without anything to eat. The winter and spring of 1933 were the most terrible. Between 1932 and 1933, nearly four million people died of hunger in Ukraine. The districts hit by the cutting-off of supplies were surrounded by troops, who prevented the peasants leaving to seek salvation in cities. Finally, food was distributed directly to workplaces, *kolkhozy* and other state companies, in accordance with the principle 'Only those who work may eat'. Workers were fed with the wheat that had been confiscated from the peasants.

In 2006, the Ukrainian Parliament officially recognised the Holodomor of 1932–33 as a genocide of the Ukrainian people. To this day, Russia refuses to acknowledge the artificial nature of the famine, which it still ascribes to a poor harvest.

5. Western Ukraine

There are two historical figures and one famous political event without which Ukraine would not be what it is today. Perhaps it would be like Belarus. Hitler and Stalin defined a different Ukraine, and, in truth, they are the ones responsible for the current protest movements. Of course, they both had their own separate plans and ideas when they sent Ribbentrop and Molotov to sign the famous non-aggression pact of 1939, the crux of which was the division of Poland.

The pact was signed, and on 17 September 1939, the Soviet army entered Bukovina and western Ukraine. It was a serious invasion, with tanks. The local population welcomed the army with curiosity, and without protest. The Galician Ukrainians were even happy, to begin with, finally to be free of the Poles, and the inhabitants of Bukovina – though not all of them, by any means – were delighted to be free of the Romanians. Within a year, however, their feelings had changed. It was true that the Poles were ejected from Lviv and Ternopil, and their houses and apartments were now occupied by Ukrainians. But not all of them: Soviet army officers and their families moved into some of those houses and apartments, and their conduct first amused, then baffled and finally frightened the western Ukrainian population.

And later, when the arrests and deportations began, the Galicians were far from happy. At that point, in June 1941, the Germans entered Galicia. They were welcomed as liberators from the communist yoke and from Stalin's repressions. Some Ukrainians applauded and went over to the German side. The nationalist organisations rose again: the same ones which had, in the 1930s, carried out terrorist acts against the Poles, and which hoped to see Ukraine end up completely independent, not only from Poland but from Russia too. Deportations – of Jews, among others – began to increase. At the same time, the Nazis led the nationalists to believe that they could count on a political quid pro quo. And it is true that Ukraine's social and cultural life flourished. Magazines and newspapers began to appear, Ukrainian theatres opened, and the hope arose of a possible Ukrainian renaissance under German occupation. Some, including Stepan Bandera, welcomed the Nazis with open arms, before later rejecting them.

At the end of the Second World War, the inhabitants of western Ukraine suffered the vengeance of the Soviet regime for their selective loyalty towards the Germans. Tens of thousands of people were deported to Siberia. But simultaneously, all over western Ukraine, a genuine partisan war began against the Soviets. There were dozens, if not hundreds, of armed groups, which ambushed Soviet politicians, soldiers and officers. The party executives sent from eastern Ukraine and from Russia were assassinated on a regular basis. As were – and this is not something that should be swept under the carpet – young rural teachers sent from Russia or

Soviet Ukraine to teach the Russian language and the communist doctrine.

This war went on until the 1960s, with tens of thousands of victims on both sides. Armed resistance to the Soviet forces was organised in western Ukraine by the Ukrainian Insurgent Army (UPA) and the Organisation of Ukrainian Nationalists (OUN). But there were also many spontaneous protests and terrorist acts against Soviet occupation.

During the Soviet era, this subject was banned, while the resistance leaders such as Stepan Bandera and the UPA commander-in-chief Roman Shukhevych were considered traitors and enemies. Since independence, however, Bandera and Shukhevych have become popular heroes again. A few rare witnesses to the events have written their memoirs and told the story of the resistance. Historians have begun to fill the gaps in the story regarding the OUN and the UPA. Dozens of books have been published, the protagonists of which have entered the history books. In western Ukrainian cities – and, soon afterwards, in cities in central and southern Ukraine – roads and monuments named after Bandera and Shukhevych have started to appear. Western Ukraine has now acquired its own heroes. Russia's reaction was intended to cause distress: Russian television channels broadcast documentary films about Ukrainian nationalists' collaboration with the Nazis, about atrocities committed by Banderites after the war, about the murders of teachers, and so on. Russia, which has traditionally exercised great influence over news and communications in eastern Ukraine, supports pro-Russian parties in the south and the east, and portrays western Ukraine and its inhabitants as enemies who betrayed the Soviet people, united in their struggle against Nazism. In the many Russian television series about the war, Ukrainians are systematically represented as traitors.

I stayed in western Ukraine for the first time in 1973, on a class trip. I was twelve years old and, although I studied Ukrainian at school, I did not speak it well. I remember an excursion to Staryi Sambir, a small town near Lviv. We were allowed to go into a shop to buy lemonade and sweets. I stood in the queue, and when it was my turn, I ordered in Russian. I remember the tense silence that filled the shop at that moment, and the hurtful words spoken to me by an old person standing behind me.

Western Ukraine was part of the USSR for only forty-six years, and it was able to keep its ethnic unity, its language and its enterprising character. The central and eastern regions of Ukraine were part of the Soviet Union as early as 1918. From my point of view, it seems impossible that this fact has had no influence on the formation of a specific mentality. In contemporary western Ukraine, small businesses and the spirit of enterprise are highly developed. The first cooperative shops and the first organisations supporting homeless people appeared in Lviv, the region's capital. The population there is much more politicised than in the rest of the country.

6. Georgiy Gongadze

Born on 21 May 1969, Gongadze was the son of Georgian film director and dissident Ruslan Gongadze. His mother, Lesya, was a Ukrainian from Lviv. After studying at the University of Lviv, Gongadze worked as a journalist and television presenter. In 2000, he founded one of the first opposition newspapers on the Internet: *Ukrayinska Pravda* ('Ukrainian Truth'). In his online articles, he proved himself a tough critic of the government, and in particular of the president, Leonid Kuchma.

On 16 September 2000, he was abducted by unknown hands while on his way home. The case received a great deal of publicity, leading to a legal inquest, personally controlled by Kuchma.

On 2 November 2000, a headless corpse was discovered in a forest, sixty miles from Kiev. The autopsy revealed that the body was that of the missing journalist. On 28 November, the leader of the Socialist Party, Aleksandr Moroz, told Parliament that he was in possession of recordings of conversations between members of the presidential administration, proving that the journalist was assassinated on the president's orders. This quickly sparked off the biggest political scandal in Ukraine since the country won its independence. The opposition, led by Yulia Tymoshenko among others, began the nationwide campaign 'Ukraine without Kuchma'. The inquest's progress was slow and erratic.

In 2003, General Pukach – from the MVD – was arrested, with the approval of the Public Prosecutor. It was Pukach who, aided by his employees, spied on the journalist before his abduction. The Public Prosecutor was immediately removed from his post, while General Pukach was freed but put under house arrest.

After the success of the Orange Revolution, the inquest into Gongadze's murder was reopened. Recordings made by Major Melnichenko in President Kuchma's office led to charges being pressed against the former Minister of Internal Affairs, Yuriy Kravchenko. On 3 March 2005, the Public Prosecutor, Svyatoslav Piskun, announced that the first interrogation of Kravchenko, regarding the Gongadze case, would take place the next day. On 4 March, Yuriy Kravchenko was found dead in his dacha. Official verdict: suicide. In spite of the fact that Kravchenko was killed by two bullets in his head.

On 21 July 2009, General Pukach was discovered in a village in the Zhytomyr region, where he had been living under an assumed name. After his arrest, Pukach revealed the place where the murdered journalist's head had been hidden. Fragments of skull were found there, and forensics analysis showed that they did indeed belong to Georgiy Gongadze.

The inquest established that General Pukach murdered the journalist on the orders of Kravchenko. On 29 January 2013, Pukach was sentenced to life in prison.

Through all these years, Georgiy Gongadze's mother refused

to acknowledge the body as being that of her son. To begin with, she said that she would not allow it to be buried until his head was found. Then she accepted burial in principle but refused to have her son's name written on the headstone. That body is still kept in a morgue. There is talk that it will be buried this year, and the journalist's mother is no longer alive to prevent it.

7. Ruslana

A Ukrainian pop singer, and the winner of Eurovision in 2004, she took part in Viktor Yushchenko's electoral campaign that year. In 2004–5, she worked as a volunteer adviser to the prime minister of the time, Viktor Yanukovych. In 2006, elected on the list of Yushchenko's party, Our Ukraine, she entered Parliament and became a deputy. But she soon gave up her political duties and returned to the stage. During the presidential elections of 2010, she was the official representative of Yulia Tymoshenko for the Lviv region. She participated actively in Euromaidan, and in March 2014, during a visit to Brussels, she called on the EU to implement sanctions against Russia following the occupation of Crimea.

8. Road Control

Founded in 2011, this is a non-governmental organisation, working to defend the rights of Ukrainian motorists against illegal police practices. Its activists film police officers breaking the law, then broadcast the videos on YouTube and use them as evidence in order to pursue legal action against the culprits, traffic control police in particular. The organisation's leader is Rostislav Shaposhnikov. Road Control activists have no legal status and act independently. Police have tried to ban the organisation several times, and its website was blocked after a court decision. Several of its members have been victims of violence and provocation.

9. Mikhail Khodorkovsky

Born in 1963 in Moscow, Khodorkovsky is an oligarch and the former CEO of the Yukos oil company. Having been the richest man in Russia, he was imprisoned in 2004 for 'large-scale fraud' and tax evasion. For some, his arrest was part of a witch-hunt against the mafia corruption that flourished under the presidency of Boris Yeltsin. For others, he was victimised politically for having dared to oppose Putin. He was released on 19 December 2013, just before the Olympic Games in Sochi, and on the 20th he left Russia for Europe.

10. Stepan Bandera

Stepan Bandera was born on 1 January 1909 in what was at the time Austria-Hungary (and is today the Ivano-Frankivsk region in Ukraine). At eighteen, he joined the Ukrainian Military Organisation (UVO), and at twenty became a member of the Organisation of Ukrainian Nationalists (OUN). In 1932, he left for Danzig, in Germany, to take classes at the German Intelligence Academy. Upon his return in 1933, he was appointed regional director of the OUN and its armed branch, the UVO.

In the 1930s, part of western Ukraine was under Polish control, and Bandera organised many terrorist actions against Polish government officials. The most famous of these actions was the assassination of the Minister of Internal Affairs, Bronisław Pieracki, on 15 June 1934. Before this attack, Stepan Bandera was arrested on several occasions by the Polish police, but released each time after a few days in custody. The murder of Pieracki led to him being arrested again and sentenced to death in 1936. Soon afterwards, his sentence was commuted to life imprisonment. He then spent four years in Polish prisons.

In 1939, he found himself unexpectedly free, following Germany's invasion of Poland. For a while, he lived in secrecy. The same year, he arrived in Krakow with a group of Ukrainian nationalists and took part in organising two Ukrainian battalions of the Nazi army, on territory invaded by the Red Army. The battalions were dissolved in 1941. Bandera did not take part in them personally.

Stepan Bandera was the ideologue of the Ukrainian nationalist movement. In June 1941, he attempted to establish an independent Ukrainian state before being arrested by the Germans, along with his comrades-in-arms. He was sent to Saxenhausen concentration camp, where the Nazis did not release him until September 1944. Bandera then remained in Germany for a time, taking maximum precautionary measures. He lived in Berlin, then went to Munich. During this period, he actively collaborated with British intelligence services.

After the war, the KGB tried to organise several attempts on Bandera's life, since he maintained his links with Ukraine's underground nationalist movement.

In 1959, a Soviet agent named Bohdan Stashynsky succeeded in assassinating him. Bandera was killed by means of a spray gun that fired a jet of poison gas from a crushed cyanide capsule. He was shot in the face as he was entering his apartment. Stashynsky was arrested by German police and admitted murdering Bandera and several other exiled Ukrainian nationalist leaders. In October 1962, a momentous trial began in Karlsruhe, the outcome of which was an eight-year jail sentence. He served his time, and was then freed. Nothing is known of his life after this.

Soviet propaganda always used the term 'Banderite' to describe all Ukrainian nationalists. Recently, Russian propaganda has taken to using this description for all Ukrainian citizens with pro-European views.

11. Ukrainian Greek Catholic Church
Founded in the sixteenth century, the UGCC is one of twenty-two eastern Catholic Churches, each with their own rites but linked to

the episcopacy in Rome. During the nineteenth and twentieth centuries the UGCC's bishops and priests actively contributed to the Ukrainian people's cultural, political and economic renaissance. Mykhailo Verbytsky (1815–70), the composer of Ukraine's national anthem, was one of them. Beyond Ukraine, the UGCC has many followers in Moldavia, Israel, Greece, Argentina, Venezuela and other countries.

Before the Second World War, the UGCC was the largest Church in western Ukraine, with nearly 2,800 places of worship, more than 150 monasteries, and its own theological academy.

After the war, the Soviet government actively repressed the Church in Ukraine, Poland and Czechoslovakia. On 11 April 1945, the KGB arrested the UGCC's archbishop, Iosyp Slipyi, and soon afterwards the entire leadership of the Church suffered the same fate. In May that year, an 'initiative group' was created, under the control of the Central Committee of the Communist Party of Ukraine and Nikita Khrushchev himself, with the aim of 'unifying the Ukrainian Greek Catholic Church with the Orthodox Church'. Khrushchev provided regular progress reports to Joseph Stalin about this unification.

In March 1946, the Soviet government organised a council in Lviv, at which the dissolution of the Greek Catholic Church was announced. All its goods were confiscated and given to the Russian Orthodox Church, while its followers and its priests were forced to publicly recant. Aleksey II, the patriarch of the Russian Orthodox Church, blessed this operation. Nearly five thousand Greek Catholic priests who refused to embrace orthodoxy were prosecuted and sentenced.

From 1946 to 1989, the UGCC continued its existence in secrecy. For eighteen years, the Church was led by Iosyp Slipyi, from the Soviet prison where he was held. In 1963, following numerous requests from the Vatican and Pope John XXIII, Slipyi was freed and expelled from the USSR. He was succeeded as head of the secret Greek Catholic Church by Vasyl Velychkovskyi, who in turn was succeeded by Volodymyr Sternyuk. Through all of this, in spite of the KGB's efforts to prevent it, the UGCC continued to be active in Ukraine, and even in Gulag camps where hundreds of thousands of believers were held, along with thousands of Church employees. In western Ukraine, new priests were trained in secret seminaries. There were even secret monasteries.

In 1989, the UGCC's followers organised mass demonstrations in Lviv demanding the legalisation of their Church. In September of that year, this point was raised during a meeting between Pope John Paul II and Mikhail Gorbachev. The Church was legalised, but the return of its confiscated possessions caused a huge number of conflicts with the Orthodox Church, which at the time was on the verge of schism.

In 2001, during a visit to Ukraine, Pope John Paul II announced the canonisation of twenty-eight New Martyrs of the Greek Catholic Church.

Today, the UGCC has places of worship all over Ukraine, including Crimea, although it is still most popular in the west of the country.

12. The language question

Ukrainian is linked to Russian and Belarusian as all three languages have the same origin. They began to divide in the seventeenth century. In 1991, the new independent Ukrainian state offered Ukrainian nationality to all residents, irrespective of their origins. Ukrainian was declared the official language and became the principal language of study in Ukrainian schools, with Russian as an option. But in reality, the country is bilingual and Russian remains strongly ingrained in the culture, particularly in the east and in the large cities. Ukrainian is still often perceived in the east of the country as a rural language.

13. Yurko Vynnychuk

Yurko Vynnychuk is a famous Ukrainian writer, born in 1952 in Ivano-Frankivsk, who now lives in Lviv. He is the founder and editor of the monthly *Post-Postup*, and a great wine lover and great hater of Yanukovych. Vynnychuk is the author of numerous novels and essays, and a popular columnist who is regularly taken to court by the heroes of his columns. In 2011, during a literary soirée, he read an inflammatory poem about Yanukovych, who was president at the time, which led to a preliminary police investigation. The offending poem was sent by the Public Prosecutor to the Institute of Ukrainian Literature (part of the Ukrainian Academy of Science) to be analysed for possibly inciting the violent overthrow of the government and the physical elimination of Yanukovych. The Institute of Literature said in its report that it had not discovered any such incitement in the text submitted to it, and had found only metaphors and other literary devices.

The police paid several visits to Yurko Vynnychuk's private residence, in order to ask him to write explanatory notes. These visits gave the police officers the opportunity to express their personal support for the author and for the ideas contained in his poem.

Andrey Kurkov was born in St Petersburg in 1961. Having graduated from the Kiev Foreign Languages Institute, he worked for some time as a journalist, did his military service as a prison warder in Odessa, then became a writer of screenplays and author of critically acclaimed and popular novels, including the bestselling *Death and the Penguin*. Kurkov has long been a respected commentator on Ukraine for the world's media, notably in the UK, France, Germany and the States.